Working with Economic Indicators

Interpretation and Sources

Donald N. Stengel and Priscilla Chaffe-Stengel

W0010462

Working with Economic Indicators: Interpretation and Sources
Copyright © Business Expert Press, LLC, 2012.

First published in 2011 by
Business Expert Press, LLC
222 East 46th Street, New York, NY 10017
www.businessexpertpress.com

ISBN-13: 978-1-60649-282-6 (paperback)

ISBN-13: 978-1-60649-283-3 (e-book)

DOI 10.4128/9781606492833

A publication in the Business Expert Press Economic and Finance collection

Collection ISSN: 2163-761X (print)
Collection ISSN: 2163-7628 (electronic)

Cover design by Jonathan Pennell
Interior design by Exeter Premedia Services Private Ltd., Chennai, India

First edition: 2011

10 9 8 7 6 5 4 3 2 1

Printed in the United States of America.

Abstract

Executives and managers hear or read headlines about recent economic data nearly every business day. Most important economic statistics are the products of programs designed to collect and analyze data to report summary results at regular intervals. Properly interpreted, these economic indicators provide useful barometers for different aspects of the economy and identify trends that aid better planning decisions. Economic indicators are available at the national level, state level, and even the regional and municipal levels.

This text focuses on economic indicators for the overall U.S. economy, identifying major categories of economic indicators and describing the key indicators in each of the categories. Most key economic indicators are reported promptly on the Internet and are provided as formatted time series that can be readily downloaded and analyzed. This text will include links to the sources for key economic indicators, as well as websites that maintain calendars of upcoming announcements and consensus forecasts of the indicators shortly prior to a formal announcement.

Keywords

Economic indicators, economic conditions, business cycles, tracking the economy, economic calendar, economic data sources

Contents

CHAPTER 1

Introduction to Economic Indicators

Value of Economic Indicators to Executives and Managers

Nearly every business day, anyone reading the business section of a newspaper or watching business coverage on a broadcast will hear reports of economic indicators announced that day and commentary from pundits as to what these indicators mean. For many of us, these reports may be just part of the information overload we encounter in the media. However, these reports generate great interest for others, whether they are market traders trying to anticipate the effect of these reports on equity and bond markets or economists who use the data from these reports to analyze the state of the economy.

While executives and managers may not need to respond to economic indicators with the briskness of the market trader or the expertness of an economist, business professionals have good reasons to monitor at least some economic indicators. These measures provide barometers on the health of the economy and potential changes in the economy, which may affect demand for the products and services their businesses and organizations provide. Likewise, some indicators provide useful intelligence about the changes in the costs their operations will face in coming months.

Beyond serving as alerts to changing conditions, values of indicators can be employed in forecasts of demand and costs, which in turn can be used to improve operational decisions. Since demand and costs are influenced by general economic conditions, many quantitative models for business forecasts include economic indicator variables to improve accuracy.

Selecting the Right Indicators and Making the Right Interpretation

In the 1976 U.S. presidential election, major candidates Gerald Ford and Jimmy Carter held two debates. In the first debate on domestic policy,[1] the incumbent President Ford stated that the U.S. economy had "added some four million jobs in the last seventeen months" and we "have now employed eighty-eight million people in America, the largest number in the history of the United States." The challenger, Governor Carter, countered, "we have two and a half million more people out of work than were when he took office." Both candidates were citing values that derive from announcements of economic indicators, yet they seem to give a different picture of the employment outlook of the U.S. economy in September 1976.

The apparent inconsistency of the economic statistics cited in the 1976 debate points out three useful reminders about economic indicators. First, different indicators may assess the same aspect of the economy from different perspectives and give different impressions. During the 25 months that Gerald Ford was president prior to this debate, the U.S. population grew by nearly 4.5 million people, with much of that increase reflected in a growth in age groups that defined the working population. Given much of the growth in the workforce at that time was from young baby boomers, it is not surprising that many of the new members of the working cohorts did not find work quickly. Hence, it is not inconsistent to have increases in both the number of people employed and the number of people unemployed.

Second, these measures need to be interpreted from an appropriate perspective. In the case of these debate statements, the changes in the numbers employed and unemployed need to be viewed in relation to the change in the working age population. The unemployment rate is one measure that reflects such a relation. When Gerald Ford took over as president, the unemployment rate was around 5.5%, and at the time of the debate, it was approximately 7.6%. (Jimmy Carter actually claimed the unemployment rate was 7.9% during the debate and may have been referring to measurements made earlier in the summer.) From the gain in the unemployment rate, it appears the increase of two and a half million unemployed supported Governor Carter in representing deterioration in the prospect for jobs. However, when Gerald Ford became president in 1974, the United States was in the midst of a significant recession that began in November 1973. The unemployment rate actually climbed from 5.5% in August 1974 to 9% in March 1975 and then began a decline to 7.6% by the time of the debate (the period of decline corresponding to the 17-month period conveniently cited by President Ford). Thus, a case could be made that the current administration had actually improved the outlook for jobs once it broke loose of the recession it had inherited.

Third, as illustrated by Jimmy Carter's inclusion of the early months of the Ford Administration (when the country was in recession) in his job loss figures and Gerald Ford's exclusion of those months in his account of job growth, it is possible to reframe a set of economic indicator data to appear good or bad by a careful selection of the time interval referenced. When studied properly, statistics can clarify, and be powerful tools of persuasion when carefully extracted and framed to support a point of view. The best defense to confusing economic reports or attempts to use statistics to promote a bias is an improved understanding of economic indicators.

Breaking News or Old News?

The noted twentieth century scholar Gregory Bateson defined information as "a difference which makes a difference."[2] This definition highlights two useful reminders when tracking economic indicators. First, not every indicator announcement makes a difference, at least not to everyone. If executives try to monitor every economic indicator, they will be overwhelmed with data, only a portion of which will be useful information. News media and business Internet sites filter the high volume of economic data and report those indicators, often with interpretations, that may be of interest to the general viewer. However, depending on the needs of the executive, the indicators selectively reported by news media and Internet sites may not satisfy the specific needs of the executive, as these media sources may neglect indicator announcements that are critical or may still include coverage of announcements that are of little value.

Bateson's definition of a piece of information as a "difference" is also a helpful reminder that these economic indicator announcements occur against a background of expectations based on earlier values of the indicator or anticipated values based on other information. As a result, the response to announcements of recent measurements can be the opposite of what might be expected if these measurements were interpreted in a vacuum. In fact, in the cases of widely tracked indicators, there are published consensus forecasts of what these values will be prior to their actual announcement.

For example, suppose the U.S. Department of Labor announces that 402,000 new claims for unemployment benefits were filed in the prior week. Without any context, this may be seen as a negative development because some people who were recently employed are now unemployed. However, if this number of new jobless claims is a lower value than the announcement for recent weeks, this most recent announcement may be a positive sign. At the same time, perhaps the consensus of economists and other professionals who track labor conditions was that the number of new filings would be only 380,000, which might make the actual announcement a negative surprise after all.

Stock and bond markets will often react to economic indicator announcements, although expectations again play a key role. The automobile industry may report that motor vehicle sales increased in one month relative to the previous month by 10,000 vehicles, but the consensus expectation prior to the formal announcement was that motor vehicle sales should increase by 30,000 vehicles. Due to disappointment relative to the consensus expectation, the prices of auto-related stocks may actually decrease following the announcement.

Economic Indicators and Economic Policy

Announcements of recent indicator values may result in a revision of expectations about economic conditions in the coming months, including the impact on economic activities and policies in the government sector. Governments can stimulate business sales and employment by purchasing goods and services, and can affect the purchasing activity of consumers and businesses by modifying tax policy. The federal government can also influence the ability of individuals and companies to borrow money, as well as influence the interest rates to be paid on debt or earned on savings.

Officials in charge of economic policy need an accurate understanding of the state of the economy in order to make effective policy decisions and have created a rich set of economic indicators for that purpose. They also study the impact of past policy measures on economic indicators in order to decide current policy measures. Often the goals of economic policy are stated in terms of those indicators. We will discuss the role of government in the context of economic indicators throughout this book, especially in chapter 9.

Investors, business managers, and other parties in the private sector are aware that government officials monitor economic indicators and formulate policy measures intended to change or stabilize future values of those indicators. These parties try to anticipate how economic policy will be altered in response to new indicator announcements and how the economy will be affected by government policy. They may decide it is in their best interests to take preparatory actions ahead of the expected economic changes, rather than wait until the changes occur. Collectively, these preparatory actions can in themselves alter the future direction of the economy.

Some economists argue that the combination of these expectations and anticipatory actions by the private sector can diminish, and even distort, the intended impact of policy actions. During the Great Depression in the 1930s, when unemployment was high and economy activity seemed chronically stagnant, the federal government broke with tradition and operated at a large deficit to spend more and pay people to work on public projects. Because this policy change was not generally anticipated, its impact was considerable in jumpstarting the economy. In the 1970s, the U.S. economy was once again facing a slowdown in the overall economy, but by then it was widely expected that the federal government would try to stimulate the economy. The anticipated policy actions helped to fuel a vicious cycle of inflation in wages and prices that unfortunately subverted the goal of stimulating the economy. Not surprisingly, during the 1970s there were formalizations of the notion that expectations of forthcoming policy changes in response to indicators will distort the impact of those policy changes.[3]

The Goal of This Book

This book provides an introduction to economic indicators. The intended audience is anyone interested in a quick orientation to economic indicators or an improved understanding of measures reported by the news and business media. The goal is to help managers and future managers use reported indicator measures to assess the condition and trend of the general economy, as well as to better judge claims and arguments posed by others on the basis of the reported measures.

The text will identify key economic indicators, organized into categories of indicators that assess similar aspects about the economy. The categories (and the respective chapters addressing each category) are:

- Indicators of economic activity (chapter 3)
- Indicators of income (chapter 4)
- Indicators of price levels (chapter 5)
- Indicators of interest rates (chapter 6)
- Indicators of resource utilization (chapter 7)
- Indicators of international exchange (chapter 8)
- Indicators of fiscal and monetary policy (chapter 9)

While not every reported indicator is cataloged in this text, the most important and widely cited measures are included.

Although economic indicators are also collected and reported for individual states, regions, and even metropolitan areas, this text will focus on measures for the overall United States for the purpose of citing actual values and illustrating the behavior of those measures in recent years. Although the United States is the focus here, similar measures are compiled and reported for other nations, groups of nations, and even worldwide by organizations in other countries or international organizations like the International Monetary Fund and the World Bank. In some cases, the names of the indicator measures may be different and the exact measurement techniques may differ significantly, but an understanding of the measures used for the United States should accelerate the understanding of economic indicators reported for other countries.

The collection of data used in the calculation of economic indicators involves complex technical issues related to statistical sampling and aggregation of data into classes. This book will not deal with all the details involved in gathering and classifying data. While these details are important for developing valid measures, most of us do not need to understand these details to appreciate the meaning of the reported values. However, a basic comprehension of how these indicators are calculated from the collected data is critical to the proper interpretation of economic indicators. Chapter 2 presents these basics, as well as provides a general understanding of how economic indicators are reported.

The Internet has become the favored medium for monitoring economic indicators and downloading economic indicator data. Access is free for indicators provided by government sources, and non-government sources provide prompt and free announcements of recent indicator values, if not access to historical data. The challenge is to access these data efficiently and effectively. The final chapter identifies some good online sources and strategies for selecting those indicators that mean the most to you.

CHAPTER 2

Fundamentals for Interpreting Economic Indicators

Before we examine key U.S. economic indicators, it will be helpful to review some fundamental concepts for interpreting economic indicators and some commonly applied techniques for adjusting and presenting economic indicator values. The chapter will also include some guidelines for tracking economic indicator announcements and preannouncement forecasts.

Economic Indicators Are Time Series

Economic indicators are repetitions of a similar measurement or counting process at regular time intervals. The intervals may be days, weeks, months, quarters, or even years. Thus, each reported value of an indicator not only provides information about the examined element at a particular time, but how the indicator value differs from the equivalent measure in prior or subsequent time intervals. Consecutive values of an economic indicator can be collected and arranged in sequence to create a set of data called a *time series*.

When indicator values are announced in the media, often only the most recent values are reported. However, the entire time series of indicators is usually available from the source of the indicator or other organizations that store economic indicators for reference. Any serious study of these indicators involves an analysis of their time series over several years.

Economic indicator data generally change over time. To understand the behavior of time series, we can look for patterns in the graph of a time series. One type of pattern is a general upward or downward change in the time series over time, called the *trend*. Upward trend often happens with time series that are affected by population growth. Another commonly observed pattern is a repeated up-and-down pattern across periods in a calendar year, called *seasonality* effects. Seasonal patterns are particularly evident when the activity reflected in the measure is affected by the time of year. Graphs of time series may also display wave-like movements that span multiple years, called *cyclic* effects. Cyclic patterns are of special interest in this text, because these fluctuations are usually associated with fluctuations in the health of the economy. Economic indicators may also be impacted by *special situations*, such as changes in behavior that occurred following 9/11. However, some fluctuations in the graphs of time series are not readily explainable by special situations and do not fit into any patterns. These are called *random effects*. Statisticians decompose time series into individual components corresponding to trend, seasonality, cyclic variation, special situations, and random effects. For more about how to identify these components, the reader might consult a text in time-series analysis.[1]

To illustrate the different components defined above, consider U.S. retail and food services sales. Figure 2.1 shows a graph of monthly values of this indicator from 1992 through 2010. First, note that although the graph does not always increase from month to month, there is a steady, upward trend in this indicator over time, broken only by a severe recession

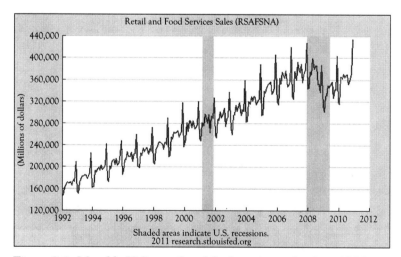

Figure 2.1. Monthly U.S. retail and food services sales from 1992 to 2010. (Source: Federal Reserve Bank of St. Louis, FRED Economic Data.)

starting in late 2007 and continuing through 2008. This general pattern occurs because the population increased, items generally became more expensive over time, and the standard of living increased so that the average household could purchase more goods and services.

If you look carefully at the graph, you will detect the repetition of a yearly pattern whereby these sales show a significant drop in January and February, followed by a slight increase in March, some slight changes through the summer, followed by a mild drop in the early fall, and finally a significant jump in December. This repeated pattern is the seasonal component for retail and food services sales. Figure 2.2 shows the seasonal pattern for months in 2010, where the value on the vertical axis is the expected seasonal fluctuation for that month relative to an average month during the year. The seasonal patterns for all months in the time series can be extracted from Figure 2.1, resulting in the graph in Figure 2.3.

If we use the values in Figure 2.3 to calculate the percent change in the retail and food services sales value relative to the same month one year earlier, the results are presented in Figure 2.4. (The months of 1992 are not represented because this series does not have data for months in 1991. Months after 2007 are omitted to be able to create this graph in a finer scale by excluding the significant year-to-year drops of the recession

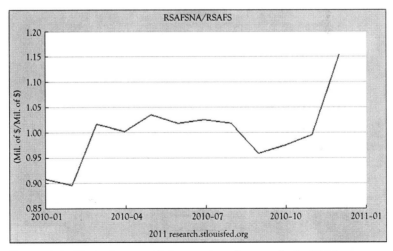

Figure 2.2. Typical seasonal fluctuations for months in 2010 as determined by the U.S. Census Bureau. (Source: Federal Reserve Bank of St. Louis, FRED Economic Data.)

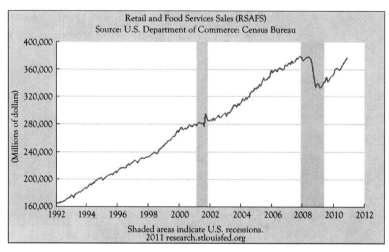

Figure 2.3. Monthly U.S. retail and food services sales from 1992 to 2010, after removing typical seasonal fluctuations. (Source: Federal Reserve Bank of St. Louis, FRED Economic Data.)

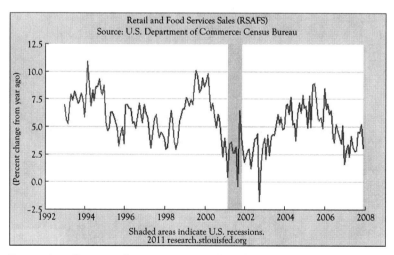

Figure 2.4. Percent change in seasonally adjusted U.S. retail and food services sales compared to the same month one year earlier, from 1993 to 2007. (Source: Federal Reserve Bank of St. Louis, FRED Economic Data.)

that followed.) Although there is some jiggle in the graph from month to month, there is a detectable cyclic pattern that climbs until 1994, drops slightly until 1998, increases again until 2000, drops considerably

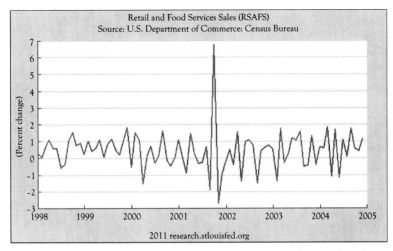

Figure 2.5. Percent change in seasonally adjusted U.S. retail and food services sales compared to the sales one month earlier, from 1998 to 2004. (Source: Federal Reserve Bank of St. Louis, FRED Economic Data.)

until 2002, climbs again until 2006, and then begins to drop again. This pattern corresponds to the business cycle for the U.S. economy, which expanded in the early and late years of the 1990s and mid-2000s, but suffered a recession in the early years of 2000s.

If we use the values in Figure 2.3 to calculate the percent change from month to month, the resulting values form the graph in Figure 2.5. The graph focuses on the months in 1998 through 2004. Note the graph moves about an average monthly change of approximately 0.4%. For the most part, up and down movements in this graph show no pattern and largely reflect random fluctuation in the time series (although there is a mild presence of the cyclic variation we noted above). However, there are noticeably larger fluctuations in the late months of 2001. The jumps correspond to the special situation of 9/11, when retail activity dropped considerably after the attack in September, when people were asked not to travel and were watching television rather than shopping. However, in October the sales jumped dramatically when consumers compensated for the cutback in purchases in September and then settled back into normal consumption patterns in November.

Growth Rates

In many instances, the magnitude of an indicator value itself conveys little information to most users. For example, if you simply reported how many billions of dollars of retail sales occurred during a month without the benefit of other information, very few people would know if the report was a positive or negative development. If you also know the level of retail sales in the prior month, you can determine whether retail sales increased or declined. While the change in retail sales from month to month would indicate an increase or decrease, the magnitude of the change also may not be that meaningful. In such cases, the indicators are often also reported in terms of *growth rates*, which are determined by dividing the change in the indicator from the previous period by the value in the previous period. Growth rates are often expressed as percents. When an indicator is increasing, the growth rate will be a positive number, and when it is decreasing, the growth rate will be a negative number.

Growth rates are often reported on an annual basis. When the periods in an indicator time series are entire years, the calculation of the growth rate as described above is the annual growth rate. However, when there are multiple reporting periods per year, the calculation of the growth rate is more complicated. One approach to estimating the growth rate for these time series is to compare a recent indicator value to the value in the same period one year earlier. However, this calculation ignores information provided by more recent measurements.

Another approach to estimating growth rate is to use the rate of growth relative to the value in the prior period and calculate an annualized growth rate based on the period-to-period growth rate. As an example, suppose retail sales in one month are 0.3% higher than the previous month. This would be the period-to-period growth rate. To annualize the growth rate, you would need to determine the compounded rate of increase if retail sales were to increase by 0.3% in 12 successive months (in other words, for an entire year). The annualized growth rate would be calculated as follows:

$$\textit{Annualized Growth Rate } (\%) = 100 \cdot (1 + 0.3/100)^{12} - 100 = 3.66$$

To summarize, then, the periodic growth rate of i written as a percentage would be annualized by raising $(1 + i/100)$ to the number of periods, n, contained in a year, then multiplying by 100 and finally netting out the base of 100. Shown algebraically,

$$Annualized\ Growth\ Rate\ (\%) = 100 \cdot (1 + i/100)^n - 100$$

Seasonality

Whether one is examining the base measurement of an economic indicator during a recent period or its growth rate from the prior period, the time period associated with the measurement or growth rate may be pertinent. As we saw earlier, U.S. retail sales are known to occur at higher daily volumes prior to the December holiday season than in the early months of the year. Retail sales are reported monthly, but not all months have the same number of days, with some months having over 10% more days than February in a non-leap year. In the case of retail sales, analysts even take into account issues like the timing of Easter and Thanksgiving when interpreting the resulting values.

When the time series of economic indicators are organized by calendar year and period within the calendar year, often one finds repetitions of a similar pattern of increases and decreases based on the time of year when the period occurs, as we did with retail and food services sales. The typical bias in the indicator value based on the period when the value was assessed is its *seasonality effect*. Analysts who prepare economic indicators usually study seasonality effects and make adjustments to indicators to remove the typical level of bias due to seasonality. The derived values are termed "deseasonalized" or "seasonally adjusted." In the example of retail and food services sales used in the beginning of this chapter, the graph in Figure 2.3 is the deseasonalized time series. When U.S. retail sales are deseasonalized, you can compare October sales to December sales and determine if retail activity is picking up after removing the typical jump that occurs from October to December. Techniques for doing these adjustments are outside the scope of this text, but can be found in a text on time series analysis.[2]

In the prior section on growth rates, we observed that one method of estimating the annual growth rate in an indicator is to compare an indicator value to the value in the same period one year earlier. The calculation is effectively deseasonalized even without formal seasonal adjustment of the time series because the seasonality effect will be similar for the two compared values. However, as noted in the prior section, this calculation disregards the information embodied in more recent measurements.

Random Effects and Special Situations

When a time series of an economic indicator has been deseasonalized, one would like to be able to look at recent changes in the value of the indicator, compare the change to the general trend in the indicator over time and conclude that the difference is a signal of the state of the economy. Unfortunately, as noted above, time series may change, even change dramatically, due to unusual situations or simply due to random fluctuation.

Before jumping to conclusions that an unexpected increase is a harbinger of a positive or negative change in the economy, one is well-advised to consider whether some other factor may be at work. Seasoned analysts look for the presence of unusual circumstances, like extreme weather, that might be the cause. Even when such causes are not readily identifiable, some analysts are cautious not to conclude a change in the economy has occurred unless a similar change in the indicator occurs for two or three more periods.

Measurement Errors

Assessing the values of economic indicators is a complex and resource-intensive task. Attempting to measure some aspect of performance in an economy where there are millions of businesses and hundreds of millions of people is so overwhelming that the values reported cannot be assumed to be exactly correct.

Due to the large number of household and business units being addressed, it would be economically, not to mention physically, impossible to include every unit, especially if timely indicator reports are desired. The data collected for assessing economic indicators are nearly always based on a sample, or a subset of the total number of units being studied. Careful design of samples using statistical methods can make the derived measurements effective in estimating what would have resulted if all units could have been included in the data collection. Further, statistical analysts can assess the likely magnitude of the deviation of the estimate from its true value, which is called the *sampling error*.

In addition to sampling error, other errors may occur that are not caused by sampling subsets of household or business units. These are called *nonsampling errors*. These may occur due to issues such as the unwillingness of sampled parties to respond, misinterpretations of questions asked on surveys, peer pressure to respond consistently with other respondents, or even errors in recording and calculating the indicators. Whereas sampling error is accepted as a typical component of the sampling process, nonsampling errors introduce biases in the resulting estimate and should be minimized.

The economic indicators reported in this text are prepared under the supervision of professional statisticians. As such, the agencies providing indicators usually provide descriptions of the methods used, the likely magnitude of sampling error, and actions taken to minimize nonsampling error.

Index Numbers

In situations where the relative change in a measurement of the economic conditions is the main concern, indicators may be presented in the form of *index numbers*. An index number is essentially the magnitude of the element of interest expressed as a percent of the value in a common reference period, called the *base period*. Sometimes the base period may actually be the average of the measure across all periods in an entire year or even across multiple years. For example, in computing the Consumer Price Index, which we will discuss later as a measure of price levels or inflation, the longstanding base period used by the Bureau of Labor Statistics has been the three-year period of 1982 through 1984.

Index numbers are also convenient when one is trying to combine several component indicator time series into a single composite time series. The well-known Consumer Price Index is intended to gauge changes in the prices of goods and services confronting consumers. However, consumers buy many items, and prices of those items do not necessarily move in tandem. Food prices may change differently than the price of gasoline, and both of those may have different growth rates than the price of housing or entertainment.

The consumer price index is an example of an *aggregate price index*. Analysts collect data on prices of individual components in each time period and then compute a single index series based on weighted sums of prices in each period, using the quantities consumed of each component as weights. It is important that the same quantity weights be applied in comparing the sum of weighted prices in any period to the sum of weighted prices in the base period. One option for weighting prices is to select the quantities of components used in a common reference year (often the base year) to calculate the index value for every year, which creates what is called a *Laspeyres index*. Another approach varies the quantity weights by assigning the amounts used in the year associated with the calculated index value, creating what is called a *Paasche index*. So, for example, if the base year is 2005 and one wants an aggregate price index value for the year 2011, the Laspeyres index value would use the quantities from the base year 2005 as weights, while the Paasche index value would use current quantities used in 2011 as the weights.

Laspeyres indexes are sometimes criticized for being unresponsive to quantity changes and overestimating price changes. Paasche indexes are likewise criticized for being too responsive to quantity changes and underestimating price changes. Hybrid techniques for quantity weighting, sometimes called *chained indexes*, have been used increasingly for composite indexes.[3]

Another complexity in developing aggregate price indexes is that not only are the quantities of goods and services consumed changing over time, but the nature of the good or service might be changing as well. For example, a typical kitchen range purchased in 2010 is considerably different from a typical kitchen range in 1990. Newer ranges are more energy efficient, more programmable, and more versatile. The change in the price of the kitchen range between 1990 and 2010 will reflect these changes in quality and technology, not merely changes in cost of making the exact same range in 1990 versus 2010. Agencies that produce aggregate price indexes will make adjustments for these changes in quality of the good or service.

If the issue of interest is the change in the quantities of several different component goods produced or consumed over time, an *aggregate quantity index* would be more appropriate. Here time series of quantities of multiple components are combined into a single time series by weighting each component by the typical price of each component and comparing the weighted total in any period to the weighted total in the base period. The Industrial Production Index, to be discussed later in chapter 3, is an example of such an index.

Real Dollars Versus Nominal Dollars

There are at least two distinct elements involved in understanding the change in a time series that is measured in dollar value. Consider retail and food services sales. The total of these sales may increase because consumers are buying more units of goods and services. This is probably what the recipient of the indicator announcement wants to learn. However, since total sales are the product of quantity times price, summed over all retail goods and services, sales may also increase because prices are generally higher than before. If the issue of concern is whether consumers are purchasing a larger volume of goods and services, it would be helpful to be able to remove the presence of changes in prices, just as the seasonally adjusted values discussed earlier remove the presence of normal seasonal changes.

To remove the impact of price changes from a time series that has measurements in monetary values, the standard practice is to adjust the quantities so the revised dollar amounts all represent the price levels in a reference or base year. A consumer price index is often used to do this. The resulting amounts are considered to be measured in *real dollars*, whereas the monetary measure prior to the adjustment is considered to be measured in *nominal dollars* (or current dollars.) The equation for calculating the real dollar measure based on the nominal dollar measure is:

$$\textit{Year k value in real dollars}$$

$$= \textit{Year k value in nominal dollars} \cdot \frac{\textit{Price index in base year}}{\textit{Price index in year k}}$$

Diffusion Indexes

Some economic indicators are developed from surveys of consumers, managers, or experts. A standard format for a survey question is whether some facet of their own activity or the overall economy has been (or will be) improving, getting worse, or staying about the same. One way to report the results of such surveyed items is the percentage of respondents who said the item of interest is getting better, the percentage who said the item is staying about the same, and the percentage who said the item is getting worse.

One means of reducing these percentages to a single value is via a *diffusion index*. Typically a diffusion index value corresponding to the percentages of sentiments in each of the three categories is calculated by adding the percentage who said the item is improving plus one-half of the percentage of those who said the item is staying about the same. Thus, a index value of 0 would mean all respondents thought the item is getting worse, an index value of 100 would mean all respondents thought the item was getting better, and an index value of 50 would mean that the same percentages thought the item is getting better as thought it is getting worse. A diffusion index above 50 would be a positive indicator, and strongly positive when the index is well above 50. An index below 50 would be a negative indicator, especially when the index is well below 50. By comparing the diffusion index to the value in prior periods, the indicator also can show a trend of more positive sentiment or less positive sentiment. The Purchasing Managers Index (PMI) provided by the Institute for Supply Management is an example of a widely followed diffusion index.

Note that diffusion indexes differ from the classic indexing of time series discussed earlier in this chapter. In the case of a diffusion index, there is often no base period. Moreover, its value is not reported as a percentage of the measure in a reference period.

Indicator Announcements, Calendars, and Forecasts

Since economic indicators are assessed at regular intervals, such as once a month, once a quarter or once a year, it makes sense that the timing of indicator announcements can be established in advance and at about the same time in the following month, quarter, or year. U.S. retail sales, for example, are usually announced around the second week of the month, and the announcement dates are established several months in advance.

Because economic indicator announcements can potentially drive the value of the stock market in the short-term, the agencies that announce economic indicators take great care to specify the time of the announcement to the minute, and then make the information widely available promptly upon announcement. The agency staffs that are responsible for developing these indicator measures are cautioned against leaking the announcements to select individuals in advance.

Major financial websites provide a convenient source for recently announced economic indicators and dates of upcoming announcements. The announcements are organized in the form of *economic calendars* that show the indicators announced on a past day or indicators that will be announced on a future day. Clicking any indicator will open a new page with a summary report on the announcement. Sources for some of the major online economic calendars are provided in the final chapter of this text.

Economic indicators may be announced and then revised in subsequent announcements. The first reported value may be a preliminary announcement that is made prior to processing all the data collected for the indicator and using estimation techniques that infer the value from partial data. When the remaining data are carefully tabulated and analyzed, revised indicators are released.

Analysts who track economic indicators do not simply wait for the announcements. Some economists actually estimate or forecast the indicator value in advance of the announcement. The average of these forecasts for any upcoming announcement is often available in conjunction with the economic calendar websites as a "consensus forecast." In some cases, these analysts are able to make fairly accurate forecasts based on past values of the indicator and the recent announcements of related indicators. However, sometimes the actual value turns out to be surprisingly different.

Investors who track economic indicators in making their decisions consider these preannouncement forecasts. When it turns out that the forecasts are considerably different from the announced value, these investors often react quickly and adjust their portfolios. For this reason, sometimes the market reaction to an indicator announcement may be the opposite of the response that a lay observer might expect. For example, if retail sales that have been adjusted for seasonality and price inflation actually increased, but did so at a much lower level than the consensus forecast, stock prices related to retail business might drop rather than rise.

CHAPTER 3

Indicators of Economic Activity

Probably the most widely shared concern about the economy among business managers and executives is whether the economy is expanding or contracting. In this chapter we will consider some of the key U.S. indicators that measure economic activity. The sales levels for some businesses may be more closely tied to the activity in the overall economy than other businesses, but nearly all businesses see their sales move higher or lower somewhat in tandem with the overall economy. Further, for these key measures, accompanying indicators are usually reported for individual sectors and subsectors of the economy, at least one of which should apply to any business.

Gross Domestic Product

Probably the most important measure of overall economic activity in the United States is the *gross domestic product*, or *GDP*. This indicator is reported on a quarterly basis by the Bureau of Economic Analysis in the U.S. Department of Commerce,[1] which releases a preliminary report near the end of the first month following the quarter. The report is revised near the end of the second month following the quarter and once again at the end of the third month following the quarter.

Since GDP is a monetary measure, it is subject to fluctuation caused by inflation, or changes in price levels. GDP is reported at annual rates, both in nominal (or current) dollars and in real dollars. Usually the reports convert GDP changes to growth rates from the prior quarter and from the same quarter a year earlier. GDP is reported by individual business sectors as well as for the economy as a whole. GDP is also measured for geographic regions within the United States. Figure 3.1 displays a graph of U.S. GDP in real dollars from 1970 to 2010.

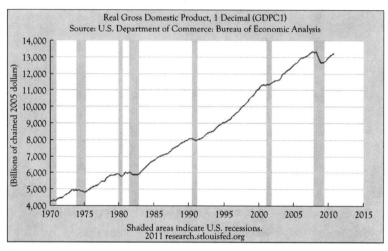

Figure 3.1. Real quarterly U.S. gross domestic product from 1970 to 2010, seasonally adjusted and annualized. (Source: Federal Reserve Bank of St. Louis, FRED Economic Data.)

The GDP for a study period represents the monetary value of all *final goods* produced during the period. Final goods represent both goods and services that are consumed rather than used primarily as ingredients in another good or service that will be sold. (Goods that are used primarily in the production of other goods and services are called *intermediate goods*.) The reason for excluding the value of intermediate goods from the calculation of GDP is to avoid double counting some components of a product or service.

Consider a loaf of bread that is available in a grocery store. A customer purchases the loaf, takes it home, where it is consumed by her household. Since the loaf is consumed, it is a final good. Prior to stocking the loaf on its shelf, the grocery store probably purchased the loaf from a bakery. Even though it was in the form of a loaf of bread, the purchase of the loaf by the grocery store would constitute the sale of an intermediate good. When the customer purchased the loaf, normally she would pay a price that is at least as high as the charge made by the bakery to the grocery store, and probably a bit higher to provide a margin to the grocery to cover part of its expenses and profits. If both the purchase by the grocery store and the customer were included in the GDP, the amount charged by the bakery would be counted twice.

In order to make the bread, the bakery needs ingredients like flour, yeast, and packaging, as well as services like labor and electricity. Since the costs of these ingredients are reflected in the price of the loaf downstream, these would also be considered intermediate goods and not included in the GDP.

Generally, goods and services purchased by individuals and households for their own use constitute final goods. When governments purchase goods and services, these purchases are usually in the form of final consumption as well. Businesses can sometimes play the role of a final consumer if the good or service is not directly included or transformed to create another good or service. For example, the bakery probably needs computers to keep track of inventory and manage accounts. The purchase of a computer and related items like software and maintenance would represent final goods in the period they were purchased.

Currently about two-thirds of the items in the U.S. GDP are purchased by individuals and households. These items are called *personal consumption*. Within those items that are personal consumption, currently about one-third are in the form of physical goods and about two-thirds are in the form of services. The fraction of personal consumption in the form of services has been increasing over time.

Government consumption represents about 20% of the GDP. This component of the GDP grew considerably as a percent of total GDP during the twentieth century, beginning in the 1930s during the Great Depression.

Approximately 12% of the GDP is final consumption by businesses and corporations. This usually takes the form of facilities and equipment needed to conduct business activities and is called *gross private investment*.

The final and smallest major component of GDP is *net exports*. This represents goods and services that are provided domestically, but consumed outside the country, or vice versa. This component may be positive or negative. The component is positive if the value of final goods and services provided domestically and consumed outside the United States exceeds the value of final goods and services provided outside the United States but consumed within the United States. Whether the amount is positive or negative is linked to whether the United States is a net exporter or net importer. While the United States was a net exporter for much of its history, during the last 50 years the country has been a net importer and the net export component of GDP has been negative. Thus, if you add the percents of GDP contributed by personal consumption, government expenditure, and gross private investment, the sum in recent years exceeds 100%, with the excess over 100% being a compensation for net imports.

Until about 20 years ago, the key measure of economy activity for the United States was a related measure called the *gross national product*, or GNP. The difference between GDP and GNP is in terms of the location and citizenship of the parties providing final goods. In the case of GNP, the measure is based on final goods provided by labor and productive assets owned by U.S. citizens, regardless of whether the production occurred on U.S. or foreign soil. The GDP is based on final goods provided by labor and productive assets located on U.S. soil, regardless of whether those assets are owned by U.S. citizens or not. The actual values of GDP and GNP are fairly equal. There has been greater emphasis on the GDP because it is consistent with the measures of economic activity used by other countries.

The Business Cycle

The U.S. GDP generally trends upward, due to increases in the population and in productivity. The rate of increase has varied, but has generally been in the 3 to 4% range in recent decades. When GDP is converted to real dollars and typical seasonal fluctuations are extracted, the graph of the deseasonalized, real GDP shows some oscillation about the general upward trend. This oscillation reflects the fact that the overall economy experiences periods of faster and slower growth (and sometimes even decline.) One common name for this oscillation is the *business cycle*.

When real GDP is in a phase of faster-than-average growth, the economy is said to be in an *expansionary* phase. When growth is slower than average, the economy is in a *contracting* phase. Often the real GDP will still increase during mild business cycle contractions because the long-term trend is positive. However, sometimes real GDP can actually decline.

When the real GDP declines in two successive quarters, the economy is commonly regarded as being in a *recession*. Officially, the designation of a recession in the U.S. economy is a determination made by a private organization called the National Bureau of Economic Research (NBER).[2] Readers will note that several of the historical graphs in this text contain shaded bars. These bars correspond to periods the NBER has deemed to be recessions in the U.S. economy.

Leading Economic Index

Real GDP provides a useful barometer of the overall health of the economy and a means of observing the current state of the business cycle. However, since most businesses make production and marketing decisions well in advance of sales, they would like to be able to forecast the future movement of the business cycle to avoid overproduction or underproduction.

One tool for anticipating the near-term behavior of the business cycle is to look at other economic indicators that have a significant cyclic component, but tend to be in an expansionary phase of that cycle in advance of real GDP entering an expansionary phase of the business cycle, and likewise tend to enter a contracting phase prior to that occurring for the business cycle. Economic indicators that demonstrate this behavior are known as *leading indicators*.

No single leading indicator can anticipate the coming changes in the business cycle perfectly. Academic researchers have identified several good leading indicators through careful analysis of time series data that tests for correlation between the cyclic component of real GDP and that of potential leading indicators in preceding months. To improve the effectiveness of using leading indicators to anticipate changes in the business cycle, multiple leading indicators can be combined into a composite index. Currently, the most widely followed composite index is the *Leading Economic Index* prepared by a non-government organization, The Conference Board.[3]

The Leading Economic Index uses a collection of ten economic indicators that, as a group, has been highly effective in anticipating recessions over the last fifty years. Specifically, the composite index arrives at a "turning point" from expansion to contraction, or contraction to expansion, about three to six months in advance of the business cycle. The economic indicators used to create this composite index are listed below:

1. Average weekly hours for workers, manufacturing
2. Average weekly initial claims for unemployment insurance
3. Manufacturers' new orders, consumer goods and materials
4. Index of supplier deliveries – vendor performance
5. Manufacturers' new orders, nondefense capital goods
6. Building permits, new private housing units
7. Stock prices, 500 common stocks
8. Money supply, M2
9. Interest rate spread, 10-year treasury note minus federal funds
10. Index of consumer expectations

Each of these indicators is described later in this book, including why the indicator acts as a leading indicator.

To illustrate the notion of a leading indicator, consider building permits for new private housing units. When a developer or general contractor wants to initiate the construction of a new house or apartment building, he will need to acquire a building permit from the local municipality and then begin actual construction activity within a certain number of days. The permit is the first step in a sequence of activities that involve employing individuals, purchasing supplies, leasing and operating equipment, and enlisting services related to selling and occupying the residential building. All of these activities contribute to economic activity.

Although the Leading Economic Index is a respected and widely followed time series, it is paradoxically of limited importance in terms of impact on the stock market. This occurs because most of the economic indicators employed in the index have already been announced ahead of the announcement of the composite index, and investors have already factored their effects into their valuations.

While leading indicators are prized for their anticipation of the business cycle, there are other economic indicators that have cyclic behavior and correlate with changes in the business cycle. Some of these indicators tend to reach a turning point in their cycles about the same time as the business cycle. These are called *coincident indicators*. There are other indicators that reach turning points some months after the business cycle and are called *lagging indicators*. The Conference Board has developed composite indexes for each of these groups. These indexes are largely of interest to economists in confirming changes in the business cycle.

Retail and Food Services Sales

The U.S. Census Bureau (part of the Department of Commerce) compiles data to estimate the total dollar value of sales of goods and services from businesses that sell primarily to the public. While a portion of these sales are made to businesses or government units, the majority of these sales are made to consumers and therefore provide a good indication of changes in the consumer expenditure component of GDP. The amount reported excludes sales taxes, credit charges, and interest.

Retail and food services sales are reported monthly near the end of the second week of the month. An advanced retail sales report is provided for selected businesses in the second week of the first following month. A preliminary report on all retail sales is provided in the second following month. A revised report is released in the third following month. The reported totals are estimates determined from samples of selected businesses that report their sales for the month.[4] Larger retailers may be included in the sample every month, while smaller retailers are included only periodically.

Retail and food services sales are reported on a nominal and real dollar basis, as well as with and without seasonal adjustment. The report is broken into major retail sectors: motor vehicles and parts, furniture and home furnishings, electronics and appliances, building and garden materials, food and beverage stores, health and personal care, gasoline, clothing, sporting goods/hobby/book/music, general merchandise and department stores, miscellaneous, and nonstore retailers (e.g., mail order). The report also includes estimates of food service sales (e.g., restaurant sales.) When this component is included, the total sales are called retail and food services sales.

Figure 3.2 shows a graph of retail and food services sales from 1992 to 2010. In chapter 2 we examined this time series in some detail, noting a fairly consistent growth trend over time, other than the recession that started in late 2007. These sales have a detectable seasonal pattern, with much higher sales in December and lower-than-average sales in the early part of the year and the initial months of fall.

Some components tend to fluctuate more than others. Motor vehicle sales are one example due to being expensive and somewhat discretionary. Because of this volatility, and since motor vehicles and parts are a sizeable component of retail sales, monthly reports usually report total retail sales excluding motor vehicle and part sales.

Likewise, food sales fluctuate considerably with random climate changes and gasoline sale revenues change considerably due to seasonality and the volatility of the crude oil market. The Census Bureau reports a general, appliance, furniture, and other (GAFO) sales total that excludes these volatile components to provide a more stable indicator of changes in retail sales.[5]

Over the last decade or so, e-commerce has become a substantial source of sales, growing from less than 1% to over 4%, and still increasing. The Census Bureau compiles a quarterly report on how much of the retail sales resulted from e-commerce.[6]

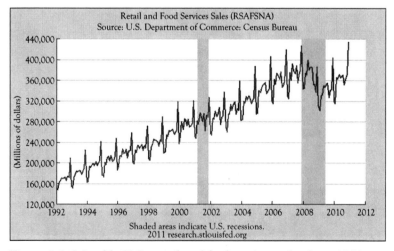

Figure 3.2. Monthly U.S. retail and food services sales from 1992 to 2010, in nominal dollars and without seasonal adjustment. *(Source: Federal Reserve Bank of St. Louis, FRED Economic Data.)*

Motor Vehicle Sales

We noted that motor vehicle sales constitute a sizeable and volatile component of U.S. retail sales. Those who track economic indicators can obtain an earlier assessment of this component in the Motor Vehicle Sales report. This report is released monthly, during the first week of the month, based on data provided by automobile manufacturers.[7]

A key item of the report is the number of units of cars and light trucks sold in the prior month, including a seasonal adjustment. The report indicates how many unit sales were from domestic manufacturers and from foreign manufacturers.

Because these purchases constitute a large and somewhat discretionary element of consumer spending, an unexpected change in the number of motor vehicle sales can signal a change in consumer spending in general and eventually in overall economic activity. Although some motor vehicle purchases are a matter of immediate necessity, often the customer already has a car or truck that could function for a while longer if necessary. When household income becomes uncertain, those who can wait to replace their vehicle often will. However, in good economic times when incomes rise and are more stable, consumers may treat themselves to a new vehicle even before the existing vehicle is worn out.

During the 1990s and the first two-thirds of the 2000s, monthly unit sales (domestic plus foreign sources) remained fairly steady in the range of 14 to 18 million. However, with the recession, collapse of consumer credit, and jumps in the price of gasoline, unit sales have dropped dramatically and have been more volatile. Figure 3.3 shows the number of lightweight vehicles sold annually from 1976 to 2010.

Industrial Production Index

While the GDP measures overall economic activity, it focuses on final goods and does not directly measure the level of activity in primary and intermediate industries. One measure that captures current activity for some primary and intermediate production is the Industrial Production Index (IPI). This indicator is a traditional index and stated relative to production in 2007, the current base year for the index. The reports

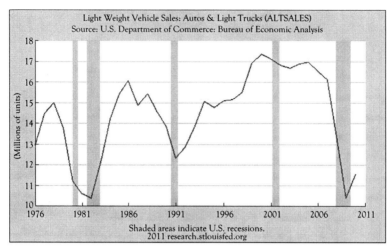

Figure 3.3. Annual U.S. light weight vehicle sales from 1976 to 2010. (Source: Federal Reserve Bank of St. Louis, FRED Economic Data.)

are prepared monthly by the Federal Reserve, with a preliminary report near the middle of the following month and revisions to the index in the reports for subsequent months.[8]

The IPI does not focus on all industrial sectors, but does include manufacturing, mining, and electric and natural gas utilities. The IPI is a quantity index, so it endeavors to measure how much production activity occurs in these sectors, not the dollar value of that production. However, in order to integrate hundreds of disparate products into a single index, prices are used as weights to create a weighted composite index. The index is also seasonally adjusted.

Like GDP, the IPI has generally increased over time but has a significant cyclic component. In fact, during a downturn in the business cycle, the IPI can decline dramatically, as it has during the recession that began in late 2007. The IPI is a coincident indicator of GDP. Although the GDP and IPI tend to have coincident cycles, it is possible for the IPI to show a strong downturn without a significant downturn in GDP or a general economic recession because other sectors that are not in the IPI may not be experiencing downturns or manufacturing firms may be using up inventories. Figure 3.4 displays both the IPI and real GDP from 1970 to 2010.

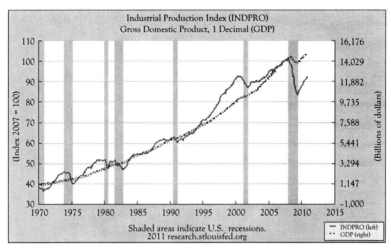

Figure 3.4. U.S. industrial production index vs. real GDP from 1970 to 2010. (Source: Federal Reserve Bank of St. Louis, FRED Economic Data.)

Manufacturers' Shipments, Inventories, and Orders

The Census Bureau surveys manufacturing firms about their activity in terms of goods shipped during a month and unfilled orders and inventories at the end of the month.[9] The amounts are expressed in dollars. To qualify as an order, there must be either a contract or firm commitment by the purchaser. The estimates are adjusted for seasonal fluctuations, including the number of days each month that manufacturers operate.

An estimate of new orders is calculated by adding the unfilled orders at the end of the month and the shipments during the month, and then subtracting the unfilled orders at the end of the prior month. Estimates of new orders are of great interest because they are indications of the change in economic activity in the coming months. Among the ten components in the Leading Economic Index discussed earlier are two categories of new orders estimates, one for consumer goods and materials and one for nondefense capital goods.

The reports on these indicators, called the "M3 reports," distinguish manufacturing activity for durable goods and nondurable goods.

A *durable good* is a good that does not get consumed or wear out quickly, such as an appliance. The formal definition is a good that lasts more than three years.

Two reports are issued for each month's data. An advance report on durable goods is issued near the end of the following month. A full report is issued in the beginning of the second month following the month being described. The amounts are broken down by the type of product. Total amounts are also reported with defense-related and transportation-related items excluded.

ISM Report on Business

Another useful set of business activity indicators is provided by the nongovernmental Institute for Supply Management (ISM).[10] The ISM conducts monthly surveys of purchasing and supply managers that pose nonquantitative questions about new orders, production, employment, supplier deliveries, and inventories. Separate reports are issued for manufacturing and nonmanufacturing businesses. The report for the manufacturing sector is released on the first business day of the next month and the report for the nonmanufacturing sector is released on the third business day of the next month.

Each survey item asks the respondent to compare an aspect of their operations that month to the prior month, and indicate whether the performance in the current month is better/higher, the same, or worse/lower. Based on the responses, a diffusion index is calculated by adding the percentage that reported a change in one direction (either better/higher or worse/lower, depending on the definition of the index), plus one-half of the percentage of respondents who said about the same. The percentages are adjusted for typical seasonal variation.

One of these diffusion indexes, the Index of Supplier Deliveries – Vendor Performance is a component of the Leading Economic Index. When this index of supplier deliveries is above 50%, supplier deliveries are slower, which indicates there is increased competition for commercial transportation services, and in turn indicates that overall business activity is picking up (which should be reflected in a few months as increased GDP).

The report combines the diffusion indexes for the individual elements to form a composite index of their activities. The composite index for the manufacturing sector is the PMI, the Production Manufacturing Index, and the composite index for the nonmanufacturing sector is the NMI, the Non-Manufacturing Index. The PMI is regarded as a useful leading indicator of corporate profits. In the past, when the PMI has dropped below 43, a recession has typically followed.

Philadelphia Fed Business Outlook Survey

The Federal Reserve Bank of Philadelphia conducts a monthly survey of manufacturing firms in their region to gauge their assessment of changes in overall business activity in the last month and the change they expect to see after six months.[11] A report is released on the third Thursday of the month and summarizes the respondents' assessments in the month of the report. In other words, the June report will report on comparisons of activity in June to activity in the preceding May and to the anticipated activity next December. Compared to other indicators, there is less time lag between the survey and the report, which increases the value of this survey.

Questions in the survey are similar to those used in diffusion indexes. Respondents are asked if general business activity, or aspects of their operations, increased, decreased, or there was no change. Unlike other diffusion indexes such as the ISM report, this diffusion index is calculated by subtracting the percent of respondents who said an item decreased from the percent who said an item increased. Thus, a positive index value suggests a consensus of increase in the item and a negative index value suggests a consensus of a decrease.

In addition to the question about changes in general business activity, respondents are asked to assess changes in new orders, shipments, unfilled orders, delivery times, prices paid, prices received, number of employees, average workweek, and capital expenditures. There are special questions that change from survey to survey. Although the survey is limited to firms in the Philadelphia region, this is a region of the United States with considerable manufacturing activity and represents a reasonable assessment of the state of manufacturing across the entire nation.

Consumer Confidence Index

Just as the ISM indexes utilize the subjective assessments of managers to gauge changes in business activity, there are indexes that assess the current and future state of business activity based on sampling consumers to assess present and future economic conditions. One such measure is the Consumer Confidence Index (CCI), which is prepared monthly by The Conference Board[12] (the same organization that provides the Leading Economic Index). The CCI report is generally released the final Tuesday of the following month. The index is seasonally adjusted.

The survey is based on a random selection of U.S. households. Surveyed consumers are asked to assess the following:

1. Business conditions now
2. Business conditions six months from now
3. Job prospects now
4. Job prospects six months from now
5. Household income for the next six months

The responses are classified as positive, neutral, or negative. A diffusion-like index is prepared for each response item by taking the percentage of positive respondents divided by the percentage of positive and negative respondents, and then multiplying by 100.

The CCI is a composite index obtained by averaging the index values calculated for the individual survey items. The resulting composite index is divided by the equivalent index in 1985 and multiplied by 100. Thus a value below 100 reflects lower consumer confidence than in 1985. The index has been well below 100 since the recession that began in 2007, even dropping below 40.

Consumer Sentiment Index

Another measure of economic activity based on consumer opinion is the Consumer Sentiment Index prepared jointly by Thomson Reuters and the Institute of Social Research at the University of Michigan.[13] Like the Consumer Confidence Index, the results are based on surveys of randomly selected households and are reported monthly. A preliminary report is provided the second Friday of the following month, with a full report at the end of the following month.

The questions in the survey are somewhat different from the CCI, but address the same basic issues about the consumer's attitude about the economy now and in the near future. The survey consists of five items:

1. Whether the respondent believes her household is better off today than a year ago
2. Whether the respondent believes her household will be better off a year from now than today
3. Whether the next twelve months will be good or bad economic times
4. Whether there will be continuous good times in the next five years or periods of unemployment
5. Whether the respondent believes now is a good time to buy big ticket items

Each response is classified as positive, negative, or neutral. An index value is created for each of the five items by taking the percent of positive responses minus the percent of negative responses plus 100. The five item indexes are totaled, divided by the index total in 1966 (the base year), and multiplied by 100.

The Consumer Sentiment Index time series tends to follow a similar pattern to the Consumer Confidence Index, although the actual values differ substantially because the indexes use different base years. Even if the difference in base years is adjusted, the two indexes may behave slightly differently due to the differences in the surveys and sampling error.

Since both the Consumer Confidence Index and Consumer Sentiment Index ask consumers to look forward and assess the future economy, these measures are leading indicators. In fact, the Index of Consumer Expectations, a subindex of the Consumer Sentiment Index, is one of the ten components in the Leading Economic Index discussed earlier in this chapter.

Housing Starts and Permits

As noted in the section on the Leading Economic Index, the commencement of constructing a new residential building triggers considerable economic activity. The U.S. Census Bureau, jointly with the U.S. Department of Housing and Urban Development, reports monthly on the number of new housing units that started in a month and the number of new housing permits that are issued during a month.[14] A preliminary report is usually issued during the third week of the following month and then reported again with revised values in the next month. Due to the highly seasonal nature of construction, the numbers are seasonally adjusted. The report breaks down housing units into single-family units, buildings with 2–4 units, and buildings with 5 or more units.

Both housing starts and permits for new housing are leading indicators for real GDP. The seasonally adjusted time series for permits is one of the ten components in the Leading Economic Index. Figure 3.5 displays the time series for housing starts from 1970 to 2010. Note that housing starts generally began declining several months before the economy was in a period of recession. Also note that the end of a period of recession often coincides with the beginning of a sustained increase in housing starts.

However, the graph of the time series displays considerable jitter due to sizeable random fluctuations from factors like extreme weather. Consequently, as is good practice with interpreting recent values for any

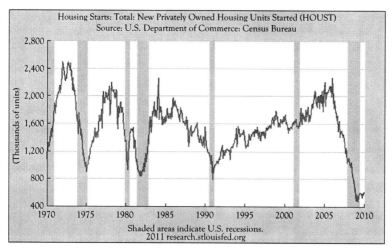

Figure 3.5. U.S. housing starts from 1970 to 2010, seasonally adjusted. (Source: Federal Reserve Bank of St. Louis, FRED Economic Data.)

economic indicator, one should be careful not to conclude a change in direction of housing starts based on values for just a month or two.

Construction Spending

The U.S. Census Bureau also tracks spending on construction once a housing unit or other building is actively being built. The report is issued the first week of the second month following the month being reported and revised in later reports.[15] Construction spending is grouped by private and public construction, as well as by residential and nonresidential spending.

Construction spending reflects an investment for a long period of time. Whether the construction is for a homebuyer, landlord, or private business, the decision to construct a building reflects confidence in the need for the facility and the ability to pay for it. As such, a dramatic increase or decrease in construction spending reflects a change in attitudes about the direction of the economy in future years.

When government entities either increase or decrease their construction spending, there is a significant *multiplier effect* on the economy. The phenomenon of a multiplier effect occurs when governmental payments for goods or services result in increased work and income for individuals. These individuals will use a portion of their income to acquire goods and services, which in turn results in additional income for other individuals, who continue the pattern of more employment and more spending. In the stimulus plan enacted by the Obama Administration in 2009, new public construction projects were a major component, based on the belief this spending would result in a significant multiplier effect that would boost the overall economy.

CHAPTER 4

Indicators of Income

In the previous chapter, gross domestic product was broken down by the type of recipient of the final goods and services: personal consumers, business, government, or net foreign. All recipients made payments for these goods and services that resulted in income to the persons or organizations in the economy who were involved in the creation of those goods and services. These income amounts are important measures in their own right, since the purchasing behavior of individuals and households is largely determined by the incomes they receive and the actions of businesses are largely determined by the profits they realize. This chapter will examine some indicators that measure incomes and profits.

Gross Domestic Income

The production of goods and services requires resources, whether in the form of labor, natural resources, or capital. In exchange for those resources, there are payments to those who provide or own the resources. When the composition of payments that result in the GDP is tabulated in this manner, the resulting total is sometimes called the *gross domestic income (GDI)*. Theoretically, GDP equals GDI, although there are usually differences in the reported amounts due to measurement discrepancies.

The Bureau of Economic Analysis (BEA) in the U.S. Department of Commerce measures GDI once a quarter as part of its reporting on gross domestic product.[1] The main breakdown of GDI is by the type of income. The following list shows the main income categories (with amounts in parentheses showing the respective percents of total GDI in 2010 for that category):

1. Compensation of employees (55.1)
2. Taxes on production and imports (6.9)

3. Net interest to domestic individuals (6.4)

4. Noncorporate proprietors' income (7.3)

5. Rental income of persons (2.1)

6. Corporate profits (8.6)

7. Consumption of fixed capital (12.9)

8. Other (0.7)

These percentages tend to fluctuate somewhat over time because employment levels, interest rates, and corporate profitability do not necessarily move in tandem.

Compensation of employees includes wages and salaries, plus supplemental amounts paid by employers during a period on behalf of employees, such as insurance. Taxes on production and imports are excise taxes, customs duties, sales taxes, property taxes, motor vehicle license fees, and other taxes on individuals. Corporate profits include dividends, undistributed earnings, and corporate taxes.

The category of consumption of fixed capital indicates a charge for replacement of aging buildings and equipment, both for private interests and government. This would include expenses recognized by businesses as depreciation.

Personal Income and Disposable Income

While GDI is the total income received in exchange for the resources that contribute to final goods and services, not all of that income comes to individuals. For example, undistributed corporate profits and replacement of fixed capital would not be income to individuals or households.

Although GDP/GDI is reported on a quarterly basis, the BEA provides a monthly measure of a portion of GDI that is received by individuals and households, called *personal income*.[2] The report is released near the end of the month following the month featured in the report, and the indicator is subject to revision in later reports.

Personal income consists of several components, or portions of components, of GDI: wages and salaries disbursed to individuals, supplementary amounts paid by employers on behalf of individuals, proprietor income, the portion of rental income received by persons, the portion of interest received by persons, and the portion of corporate dividends received by persons. Personal income is adjusted to reflect "transfer payments," which are amounts received by individuals for reasons other than employment or use of resources. Examples include payments from Social Security, Medicare, welfare, and unemployment insurance. However, payments made by individuals to programs like Social Security and Medicare are netted out in the computation of personal income.

The personal income report is of considerable interest because income is related to consumer and business spending, which drives economic activity and indicates future directions for corporate profits and borrowing. However, not all personal income is available for spending because individuals must pay taxes on income and property. The monthly BEA report estimates these taxes and subtracts them from personal income to determine *disposable personal income.*

Figure 4.1 provides graphs of personal income and disposable personal income on an annual basis from 1970 to 2010 in real (2005) dollars. Although both time series move roughly in proportion, the graph shows disproportionate narrowing and widening corresponding to changes in tax laws and different average tax rates.

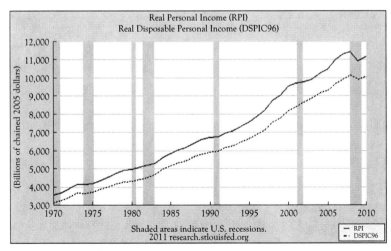

Figure 4.1. Annual U.S. personal income and disposable personal income, in real (2005) dollars, from 1970 to 2010. (Source: Federal Reserve Bank of St. Louis, FRED Economic Data.)

Personal Outlays and Personal Consumption Expenditures

Most of the disposable income received by individuals and households is spent on goods and services. As part of the monthly report on personal income, the BEA estimates these expenditures, which are termed *personal outlays*.

The estimated amount for personal outlays is approximately equal to the GDP component that estimates the value of final goods to individuals and households, called *personal consumption expenditures*, or PCE. The difference in these amounts is that personal outlays include personal interest payments (interest on personal debt rather than mortgage debt) as well as donations and nontax payments to governments, whereas the PCE amount does not.

Personal Saving

Individuals do not spend all of their disposable income. Some is set aside for future consumption, protection for possible loss of income in the future, or as a means of increasing future income through investments. The BEA calculates *personal saving* as the difference between disposable income and personal outlays in a period and provides this as part of the monthly report on personal income and outlays.

Personal saving is typically reported in terms of a percent of disposable personal income. Figure 4.2 displays the personal savings rate since 1959. The graph shows a dramatic change in the savings rate, which was much higher in the 1960s and 1970s. Part of the reason for this drop has been the dramatic growth in the value of stocks and real estate. The gains in these assets, even when not realized by sales, had a "wealth effect" that gave many consumers confidence to spend more of the money they earned in wages and salaries or had saved in checking and banking accounts. Note that the savings rate jumped in the early 2000s following the collapse of stocks in the dot-com bust, then slid back to record lows of almost zero, until jumping again after the joint collapse of the real estate market and stock market starting in 2007. Even so, the savings rate is still roughly half of what it was 40 years ago.

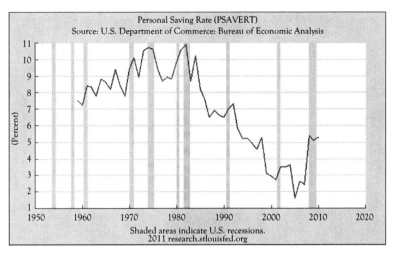

Figure 4.2. Annual U.S. personal savings rate from 1959 to 2010.
(Source: Federal Reserve Bank of St. Louis, FRED Economic Data.)

Corporate Profits

Corporations obtain revenue from sales, but much of that revenue is used to cover expenses for employment, borrowing funds, acquiring resources, and making payments to maintain its own property. The difference between revenue and expenses is a firm's profit (or loss if the difference is a negative number.) Some of the profit is taxed by governments, some is paid to equity shareholders (individuals, other corporations, and foreign sources), and some is retained to invest in future growth.

The BEA provides a report on overall U.S. corporate profits on a quarterly basis along with its quarterly GDP reports. A preliminary report on corporate profits is announced near the end of the second month following the end of a quarter and is revised near the end of the third month following a quarter.

Figure 4.3 shows a graph of annual corporate profits and GDP from 1970 to 2010 on separate scales. Note that corporate profits fluctuate considerably more than GDP. Also, corporate profits tend to decline a few years prior to a major recession while GDP will increase up to the beginning of a recession. Also, corporate profits often begin increasing before a recession ends.

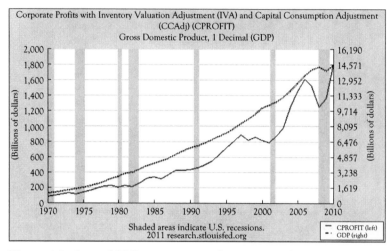

Figure 4.3. Annual U.S. corporate profits vs. gross domestic product from 1970 to 2010. (Source: Federal Reserve Bank of St. Louis, FRED Economic Data.)

Corporate Earnings Reports

While there is a clear positive relationship between corporate profits and overall economic activity, the corporate profits announcement tends to offer little new insight to investors. Since most corporations are publicly owned, they are required to make quarterly reports of their earnings and other financial results. Thus, when the BEA announces its value of corporate profits, most investor institutions already have a fairly good idea what the collective profits will be.

Although these quarterly earnings reports from corporations are not technically economic indicators, many are followed and anticipated by a wider audience than current investors and potential investors. Some large companies are regarded as bellwethers for their industries. As such, the changes in revenue and earnings for a large company can provide an advance estimate of revenue and earnings for the entire sector to which it belongs.

If the industry sector represented by a major company is a sector seen as a driver of economic activity, quarterly earnings reports can have the effect of a leading indicator for changes in broader economic measures like GDP. For this reason, a single earnings report can have a strong effect on the broader stock market.

Earnings reports can also confirm or contradict changes that are suggested by traditional economic indicators related to that industry. Since all time series are subject to random fluctuations and usually have some sampling error, the indicators may be misleading. Corporate earnings reports provide additional data that can confirm or contradict changes in reported economic indicator values.

Just as economists offer forecasts of conventional economic indicators before the actual formal announcement, industry analysts often forecast the earnings of corporations ahead of the earnings reports. Average estimates and ranges of estimates are widely available on the Internet. Some firms often contribute to these forecasts by offering formal earnings "guidance."

Stock Market Indexes

Probably the most frequently reported items in a business report are the changes in stock market indexes like the Dow-Jones Industrial Average, the S&P 500 index, and the Nasdaq market index. Like corporate earnings reports, these reports are of great interest to investors. As measures of overall changes in the prices of traded stocks, these stock market indexes provide good real-time indications of changes in the value of an investor's portfolio of stocks and even a reasonable estimate of percentage changes in the value of individual stocks.

Since owning a share of stock gives an investor the right to share in future earnings of a corporation, a change in a broad stock market index is an indication of change in the collective wisdom of many investors as to the profitability of corporations in the future. As documented in James Surowiecki's book, *The Wisdom of Crowds*,[3] large groups of people with varying levels of expertise are often collectively better forecasters than small groups of recognized experts. And since corporate profitability is linked to economic activity in general, general stock market indexes behave as a leading indicator of GDP. One of the major stock market indexes, the S&P 500, is one of the ten components in the Leading Economic Index.

Whether corporate profits translate directly to personal income or are retained for future growth is governed by the dividend policies of corporations. The financial industry regularly publishes the dividend rates corresponding to major stock market indexes. Dividend policies are strongly influenced by tax laws, such as whether dividends are taxed as ordinary income or as capital gains. During the stock market boom of the late twentieth century, many corporations paid at low dividend rates because dividends were taxed as ordinary income. However, with the change in the tax laws in the last decade that allow dividends to be taxed like capital gains, there has been a return to higher dividends.

Distribution of Income

Indicators of income and savings on the national level imply changes in future spending and economic activity, but the nature of that spending and economic activity will depend on how income and savings are distributed across different age groups, ethnic groups, and areas of the country. One means of assessing the distribution of income is from an annual report issued by the U.S. Census Bureau, called *Income, Poverty and Health Insurance Coverage in the United States*.[4] This report is available in the fall of the following year.

The report is based on results of the American Community Survey that includes a large sample with attention to adequate representation across multiple demographic classifications. This effort is conducted in conjunction with the Census Bureau's ongoing work to monitor population changes for the decennial census report.

In addition to reporting median household incomes for various demographic sectors, the report offers a glimpse into variation in household incomes. The report includes a table showing how total household incomes are distributed among five quintiles of the population, ranked by household income. In 2009, the quintile of households with the lowest income received 3.4% of total household income, while the top fifth received 50.3%. The report also includes some summary measures of income inequality, including the Gini index.[5] The Gini index is a value on a scale from 0 to 1, with 0 representing total equality and 1 representing maximal inequality. The Gini index for the United States has been climbing in recent decades, from 0.386 in 1968 to 0.468 in 2009.

The report also estimates and compares wages and salaries for fully employed individuals. While earnings for both men and women have increased in real dollar terms, the ratio of average earnings of female workers to male workers has increased from around 60% to around 77% over the last 50 years.

Millions of households have incomes that fall below the poverty threshold calculated by the Census Bureau. In addition to the political and social aspects of poverty, the preponderance of poor households has economic implications in terms of macroeconomic policy. After a significant decline in the 1960s due to changes from Great Society programs, the poverty rate in the United States has generally remained in the range of 12 to 15%.

Distribution of Wealth

While current income is the main source of funds to cover the expenditures of most households, households often accumulate savings by having smaller outlays than income, receiving inheritances, and resulting from gains on investments of those savings. The accumulated savings, or wealth, is stored for future periods when outlays could exceed income, such as in retirement years. The distribution of wealth is not identical to the distribution of income in the population. In fact, there is greater inequality in wealth than in annual incomes.

The Federal Reserve has done an assessment of the distribution of household net worth every three years, starting in 1989, based on data from the Survey of Consumer Finances that it sponsors. Between 4000 and 5000 households were sampled in recent surveys. Reports appear in the second year following the year of the study. The most recent reports at the time of this writing were in 2009, reporting on 2007 and earlier years.[6]

Household or family wealth is reported for different demographic groups in terms of median wealth and mean wealth. Since the distribution of wealth is skewed with most households on the lower side and relatively few in the upper tail, mean wealth is typically higher than median wealth. The degree of disparity between median and mean household wealth is an indication of wealth inequality. In 1998, median family net worth was 91.3 thousand dollars (measured in 2007 dollars) and mean family net worth was 359.7 thousand dollars. In 2007, the median and mean increased to 120.3 and 556.3 thousand dollars, respectively. The fact that the mean grew a faster rate than the median is an indication of an increase in wealth inequality over that period.

The analysts for the Federal Reserve study use deciles to divide households when ranked according to family wealth. Between 1998 and 2007, there was little change in real median wealth for the bottom 40% of households, while families between the 60th and 90th percentiles had median wealth increases of almost 50%, and the top tenth of households based on wealth had their median net worth nearly double. The results reflect that the middle class is not enjoying the same relative gains as wealthier households. The recent report also reflects greater relative increases in wealth for families where the heads of household are older. However, these changes correspond to years before the recent recession, and the upcoming report for 2010 may change these trends.

Household Net Worth

The Federal Reserve System maintains a set of accounts that keeps track of the flow of funds between different sectors in the economy and balances of those accounts. These quantities are reported quarterly near the beginning of the second month after the end of the quarter.

One sector in the report corresponds to households. A balance sheet for households (including nonprofit organizations) estimates the total assets, total liabilities, and net worth at the end of the quarter for this sector.[7] Assets are itemized into categories, including real estate, durable goods, bank deposits, amounts in credit instruments (like bonds), amounts in corporate stock and mutual funds, and reserves in pensions and life insurance. Liabilities include balances on mortgages and other types of loans.

Figure 4.4 shows the total net worth of household and nonprofit organizations between 1950 and 2010. The total net worth of households grew steadily at a geometric rate until the beginning of this century when the dot-com crash wiped out a considerable amount of wealth held in corporate equities. A larger drop in net worth occurred in the recession of 2008 and 2009, when both corporate equities and net equity in real estate tumbled.

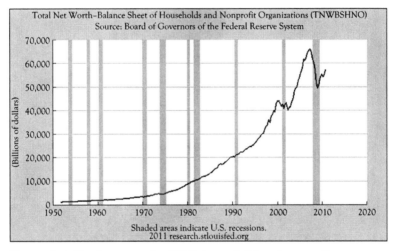

Figure 4.4. Total net worth of U.S. household and nonprofit organizations from 1950 to 2010. (Source: Federal Reserve Bank of St. Louis, FRED Economic Data.)

CHAPTER 5

Indicators of Price Levels

Prices of goods and services change. Sometimes the cause of the change is a temporary imbalance between supply and demand. When there is excess demand relative to supply, there is an upward pressure on the market price, and when supply exceeds demand there is a downward pressure on price. Since prices must be sufficiently high to cover costs for a business to sustain its operations, but not so high as to lose business to competitors, the price a firm will charge is affected by changes in the prices it must pay to acquire the labor, raw materials, energy, and other resources needed to provide its product or service. Consequently, price changes in one sector of the economy spill over to other sectors. Further, as we will discuss in chapter 9, macroeconomic policy can affect price levels. This chapter deals with economic indicators that monitor changes in prices.

Inflation

The economy is a largely closed system whereby the providers of resource inputs to one sector of the economy are also either directly or indirectly purchasers from the sectors to which they sell. As we saw in the previous two chapters, consumers are both the largest recipient group of final goods in GDP and the group receiving most of the income from the creation of final goods in the GDP. When the prices that consumers pay increase substantially, incomes must increase for consumers to be able to continue to acquire the goods and services they need. The increase in incomes, in turn, puts more cost pressure on the goods and services that require labor, resulting in a positive feedback loop. For this reason, prices for most goods and services tend to move in tandem.

When purchasers in an economy generally have to pay more to acquire the same physical goods and services, there is said to be price *inflation*. When the costs of acquiring the same physical goods and services decrease, there is said to be price *deflation*. The rate of inflation is usually expressed as the percent increase on an annualized basis. (In the case of deflation, the rate is usually expressed as a negative percent increase.)

We will discuss the role of inflation in macroeconomic policy in chapter 9, but here we can say that when the rate of price inflation is high and uncertain, inflation itself creates turmoil for the economy. In making decisions on capital investment and business strategy, most businesses need to anticipate the future prices they will receive for the goods and services they sell and how much they will pay for the goods and services they buy, even years in advance. When inflation is high and uncertain, projects that require investment of resources look very risky and firms may hold back from investment as a result. Also, when inflation is high and uncertain, both firms and employees will endeavor, if possible, to increase the prices for the goods and services they provide, not only to compensate for recent increases in prices they pay, but in anticipation of even higher costs they expect to face in the near future, thereby stirring more price inflation.

In this chapter, we will consider some important indicators of price levels that help determine the degree of price inflation present and whether inflation is increasing or decreasing. Initially, we will address some broad indicators that reflect general price level changes. Next, we will examine some indicators that track the prices of key goods or sectors of the economy.

The Consumer Price Index

Probably the most widely reported measure of general price levels in the United States is the *Consumer Price Index*, or CPI. The intent of the index is to provide a relative measure of prices faced by consumers in one time period compared to other time periods. Prices are weighted by amounts of each item that are used by a typical household, called a "market basket." The index is prepared by the Bureau of Labor Statistics (BLS) in the U.S. Department of Labor, which reports new index values on a monthly basis. Reports are issued near the middle of the month following the month of the report.[1]

The BLS actually prepares two CPI indexes: The CPI-U tracks general price levels for urban consumers, which represents about 87% of the U.S.

population. The CPI-W tracks price levels for wage earners, which represents about 32% of the population. Both indexes use the average prices over the three-year period from 1982 to 1984 as the base period values. Indexes are reported for four regions of the nation (northeast, midwest, south, and west) and several metropolitan areas.

Reports are usually cast in the form of percent increases from the prior month and percent increases from one year earlier. Values are reported with and without seasonal adjustments. Figure 5.1 shows the annual average CPI-U from 1970 to 2010. Figure 5.2 shows the year-to-year percent change in the CPI-U for the same period. The values in the second graph provide an estimate of inflation rates faced by urban consumers.

The composition of the market basket is determined from the Consumer Expenditure Survey. This composition changes over time due to changes in what consumers buy. For example, over the last century, consumers have changed from eating relatively higher amounts of pork, to relatively higher amounts of beef, and later to relatively higher amounts of chicken.

The monthly reports also provide indexes for prices of the individual items in the market basket, as well as the percent month-to-month and 12-month changes in the prices of those items. Prices of some of

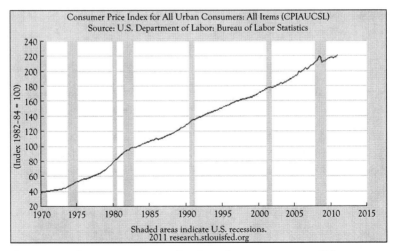

Figure 5.1. Consumer price index for urban consumers, all items, seasonally adjusted, from 1970 to 2010. (Source: Federal Reserve Bank of St. Louis, FRED Economic Data.)

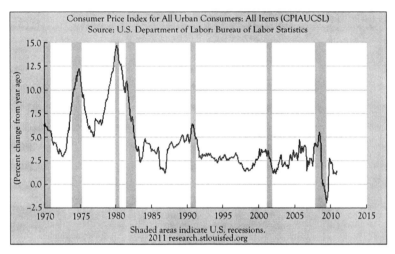

Figure 5.2. Percentage change from one year earlier in consumer price index for urban consumers, all items, seasonally adjusted, from 1970 to 2010. (Source: Federal Reserve Bank of St. Louis, FRED Economic Data.)

these components are more volatile than others. Items related to food and energy tend to fluctuate more due to the random effects of weather on food and the impact of political events on foreign supplies of crude oil. The CPI measures are reported with food and energy items excluded to form what is called a core CPI. This measure is more stable and often cited as a better indicator of inflation in consumer prices.

The percentage change in the CPI is sometimes used to estimate changes in the cost of living. Many programs, including federal government programs like Social Security, use the CPI-U as the basis for adjusted payments from year to year. The CPI-U is also the basis for adjusting income brackets for individual U.S. income taxes.

However, the BLS states that CPI is probably an upper bound for the change in the cost of living, because it does not account for consumer decisions to substitute consumption in response to price changes so as to get more utility per dollar of expenditure. The BLS has started reporting a Chained CPI-U that better accounts for this substitution.[2]

During the last century, the CPI was criticized for not reflecting quality changes in a commodity. For example, a television set purchased in 2011 has different features and quality than a television purchased in 1982. In some cases, items are no longer sold and have been replaced with similar, but not identical items. The BLS has developed a technique called a hedonic quality adjustment to try to address this issue and has been expanding the use of this adjustment to a wider array of goods and services.[3]

The PCE Price Index

The Bureau of Economic Analysis, in conjunction with its data collection, analysis, and reporting of personal income and outlays, provides another index of inflation in consumer prices. Since this index is based on expenditures on the items included in the personal consumption expenditures component of GDP, it is known as the *PCE Price Index*. Like personal income and outlays, it reports the index on a seasonally adjusted monthly basis, with 2005 as the base year. However, the new value is usually expressed in terms of the annualized percent increase from the prior month. The monthly percentage change in the index excluding food and energy is announced as well.

The PCE price index appears to be measuring changes in same set of consumer prices as the CPI. In fact, in preparing the PCE, the BEA uses data from the Bureau of Labor Statistics, which produces the CPI. Month-to-month changes in the PCE price index are often close to the CPI-U, as shown in Figure 5.3 for years from 1970 to 2010. One reason for any difference is that while the CPI is based on prices paid directly by consumers, the PCE price index includes expenditures by nonprofit organizations on behalf of individuals. Another source of difference is that the weights assigned to components in the PCE price index change from month to month to reflect changes in purchasing patterns, while the CPI only revises the expenditure weights every two years. (However, the methodology used in calculating Chained CPI-U does reflect period-to-period changes in purchasing patterns.)

The PCE price index has received increased attention due to a belief that the Federal Reserve places greater trust in the PCE index than the CPI-U as an indicator of inflation. Analysts and investors who are trying to guess how the Federal Reserve will act in its next meeting use the PCE price index reports as a basis for those guesses.

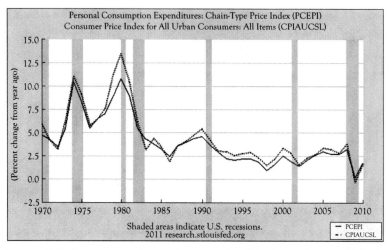

Figure 5.3. Percentage change in annual PCE price index vs. CPI-U, seasonally adjusted, from 1970 to 2010. (Source: Federal Reserve Bank of St. Louis, FRED Economic Data.)

The Producer Price Index

The CPI and PCE price indexes focus on final goods that are directed at consumers. While prices for other goods and services in the economy mirror the general movement in consumer prices, there are differences in timing and magnitude. Since consumer price changes are driven by changes in production costs, price changes may occur first in basic materials and intermediate goods before being manifested in final consumer goods. Some firms have "pricing power" that allows them to pass along cost increases in the form of higher prices, even in a weak economy, without suffering a significant loss in sales volume. However, in times when the consumer demand is soft, it is possible for prices of some basic materials and intermediate goods to rise without being passed along a price increase to the consumer.

To track prices across the economy at all stages of production, the Bureau of Labor Statistics compiles a monthly *Producer Price Index* (PPI).[4] The index is built from individual price indexes for thousands of goods and services, with recent values of the index and month-to-month changes of each in the detailed monthly report. The BLS uses 1982 as the base year for prices, but updates quantity weights every five years to reflect changes in the economy. The report is issued near the middle of the month following the month featured in the report.

In addition to providing a total producer price index, goods are classified as being finished, intermediate, or crude. Finished goods are goods for which processing is complete and are ready for distribution or sale. An example would be an automobile that has completed assembly. Intermediate goods are those where some processing is complete, but there is additional processing to go. A manufactured part that has no value as a good in itself, like a dashboard for a car, would be an intermediate good. Crude goods are goods that have been extracted via farming, forestry, or mining, but not processed.

Figure 5.4 shows the PPI components for finished goods and crude goods on the same graph from 1970 to 2010. Clearly there is more fluctuation in the price index for crude goods than finished goods, with the spikes corresponding to periods when there were spikes in oil prices. Crude goods are based more on commodity prices and less on labor costs than finished goods.

The monthly report provides individual producer price indexes for 15 major sectors of the economy. The portions of the PPI related to food and energy are reported separately, and those components are extracted

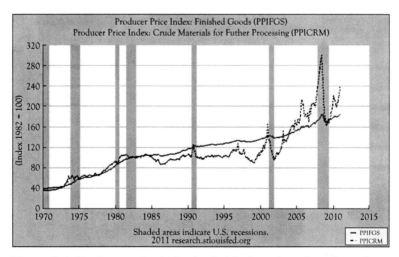

Figure 5.4. Producer price index for finished goods and crude goods, seasonally adjusted, from 1970 to 2010. (Source: Federal Reserve Bank of St. Louis, FRED Economic Data.)

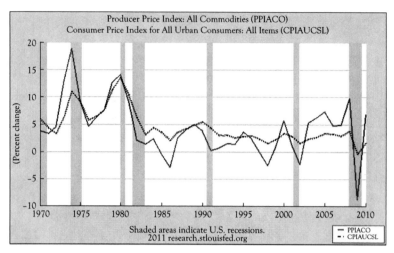

Figure 5.5. Average annual percent change in PPI and CPI-U, seasonally adjusted, from 1970 to 2010. (Source: Federal Reserve Bank of St. Louis, FRED Economic Data.)

from the total PPI to provide a core PPI. As with the CPI and PCE Price Index, the lead report on the PPI is expressed in terms of percent change from the prior month and seasonally adjusted. Also, since the PPI tracks prices of individual items and those items are periodically replaced or updated with similar items of different functionality, the BLS makes quality adjustments to some item indexes.

A graph showing year-to-year percent change in the PPI from 1970 to 2010, compared to the CPI, appears in Figure 5.5. Note that the changes in the CPI largely track the changes in the PPI, though not exactly. Again, there are good reasons to expect the indexes to track closely: consumer prices are related to the costs of producing consumer goods and many of the finished goods in the PPI are intended for personal consumption. The PPI sometimes moves slightly in advance of the CPI, particularly when the CPI is compared to the PPI indexes for crude or intermediate goods.

The GDP Deflator

The data collected by the Bureau of Economic Analysis to calculate the PCE price index is part of a broader ongoing project to collect data on prices of all final goods in the U.S. domestic economy. These efforts are necessary to be able to express GDP and GDP components in terms of real dollars (currently with 2005 as the base year.) The basis for converting GDP to a real dollar amount uses a chained price index that, as with the index used in the PCE price index, better responds to substitution than price indexes like the CPI and PPI, which use fixed quantity weights to aggregate the price changes of individual items into a single index.

The ratio of the GDP in nominal (or current) dollars in a period to the associated real dollar value in that period creates an index-like measurement called the *GDP deflator.* By examining changes in the deflator from one quarter to the next and then annualizing the change, one gets an estimate of the inflation rate for all final goods in the economy.

Although the GDP deflator reflects price changes over a wider range of final goods, the deflator closely tracks the PCE price index. Since the PCE price index is estimated on a monthly basis and the GDP deflator is estimated quarterly, the PCE price index tends to receive more attention in the business media.

Average Hourly Earnings

Labor is generally a dominant expense for businesses, and wages and salaries are the main source of income for most households. If wages outpace consumer prices, households can either increase savings or increase consumption. If consumer prices outpace wages, consumers will either reduce savings or consumption. The wages and salaries received by an individual are the product of the number of hours worked and the rate of earnings per hour. We will examine an indicator of the number of hours worked in chapter 7. For a typical person fully employed at 40 hours per week, change in earnings per hour reflect changes in that person's income from wages and salaries.

The Bureau of Labor Statistics releases a report called *The Employment Situation* in the early part of each month.[5] One item in that report is the average hourly earnings of employees on nonfarm payrolls in the previous month. While not a formal index, it can be used as an index of the average earnings corresponding to an hour of employed labor. The report states the change in earnings per hour in monetary amount and percent change.

The BLS started reporting average hourly earnings of all employees on nonfarm payrolls in 2006. This indicator expands the base of employees represented in another monthly BLS time series that measures average earnings of production and nonsupervisory employees of private businesses. Interestingly, average hourly earnings for production and nonsupervisory employees in private businesses have climbed at a fairly steady rate over the last 30 years. The increase continued even during periods of recession, when unemployment increased, and there was an excess supply of labor.

The Employment Cost Index

From the perspective of employers, compensation of employees is wages and salaries plus benefits. The Bureau of Labor Statistics prepares a quarterly employment cost index to track these components.[6] The index uses 2005 for a base year and is seasonally adjusted. The report appears at the end of the month following the end of the quarter.

The report also separates the employment cost index into a wage and salary index and a benefits index. A graph of these separate indexes from 2001 to 2010 appears in Figure 5.6. Note that the cost of benefits rose faster than wages in the first five years.

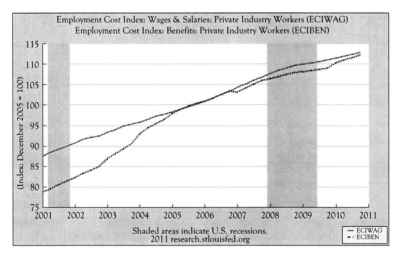

Figure 5.6. U.S. Employment cost index for wages and salaries and employment cost index for benefits, private industry workers, seasonally adjusted, from 2001 to 2010. (Source: Federal Reserve Bank of St. Louis, FRED Economic Data.)

The detailed report provides separate employment cost indexes for employees in private firms and employees of government. There are also separate indexes for major private sectors.

The S&P/Case-Shiller Home Price Indices

In studying changes in home prices, economist Karl Case developed a method for estimating the rise in home prices looking at repeat sales of homes. Based on an impression that the rise in home prices was not sustainable, he worked with economist Robert Shiller, and the two concluded there was a housing market "bubble" prior to the collapse of residential real estate prices in the first decade of this century.

Case and Shiller expanded their research into an ongoing program based on a modification of their repeat sales methodology with monthly reports that are published by Standard & Poors.[7] Data are collected from 20 metropolitan areas. In addition to price indices for each area, there is a 20-city composite index that uses 2000 as the base year. Cities are weighted by the relative value of real estate in each metropolitan area. The composite index for 20 cities begins in the year 2000. Originally data were collected in 10 of the metropolitan areas. There is a composite index reported for these 10 areas that dates back to 1987.

While the index and changes in the index are reported monthly, the index is actually based on a three-month moving average of repeat sales data. The indices are published on the final Tuesday of the second month following the month featured in the report. Houses that undergo substantial change after the initial purchase are excluded to avoid problems with changes in quality. The analysts also remove repeat sales that do not involve two sales that are both arm's length exchanges between private parties.[8]

Sales Price of Existing Home Sales

The National Association of Realtors maintains a considerable database of existing homes that sold or are available for sale. This organization offers a public report toward the end of every month summarizing sales of existing homes and pending home sales.[9] Sales are reported for different regions of the country (northeast, midwest, south, and west). Single-family homes and condominiums are reported separately. Sales prices are reported by median price and average price.

While the S&P/Case-Shiller report provides a reliable guide for the rate of change in home prices by its focus on repeat sales, the report from the National Association of Realtors provides a readily understandable measure in terms of the typical price.

The report also includes counts of the home sales, both seasonally adjusted and not adjusted. While existing home sales do not involve the same level of production activity as a new home, an increase in sales does portend additional economic activity in terms of renovation work and new appliances. As a major capital expense, an increase or decrease in home sales also serves as an indicator of consumer confidence.

The inventory of unsold homes-for-sale is identified and expressed in terms of the number of months of supply at the expected rate at which houses will sell. In the aftermath of the bust in home prices and rise in mortgage defaults, there has been over 12 months of supply of existing homes.

Price of New Houses Sold

The Bureau of the Census compiles data on new home sales similar to what the National Association of Realtors provides for existing home sales. A report is issued monthly, usually shortly after the National Association of Realtors' report.[10] The figures are subject to revisions in subsequent monthly reports.

Figure 5.7 shows the median price of new houses sold in the United States from 1963 to 2010. Note that during most recessions (indicated by the darker bands), median housing price increases stalled, but did not decrease much. However, in the recession that began in 2007–08, the median price of new homes sold dropped around 20%, and has only increased slowly.

In addition to the median and average prices, the report provides a distribution of how many new homes sold in various price ranges. The report includes counts of homes sold, seasonally adjusted and not adjusted, the median time a sold new home was on the market, and the number of new homes for sale at the end of the reporting period.

Figure 5.7. Median price of new houses sold in the U.S., monthly and not seasonally adjusted, from 1963 to 2010. (Source: Federal Reserve Bank of St. Louis, FRED Economic Data.)

In chapter 2 we discussed the presence of random fluctuations in time series. We cautioned that the magnitude of these fluctuations can sometimes be large enough to lead to a wrong conclusion about the direction in which an indicator is moving. This caution is particularly pertinent in looking at a single month-to-month change in any of the indicators for housing prices in the last three sections, particularly when applied to individual metropolitan or county markets. The National Association of Realtors has local affiliates that prepare the same indicators for existing home sales in their territory as the national parent does for the nation. Due to the relatively small number of sales in these territories, there can be considerable random fluctuation, even in the median selling price.

Oil Price

In the 1970s, the United States learned painfully how dependent it had become on petroleum. Despite the fact that the world oil industry started in the United States, by the 1970s the amount of the petroleum drilled domestically became substantially less than the amount consumed domestically. As the result of the exercise of market power by countries that exported oil and political problems in the Middle East, the price of crude oil jumped dramatically after a long stable period when crude oil had remained about $3 a barrel. Oil ratcheted first to prices above $10 and then to almost $40 by 1980. The price per barrel dropped and remained around $20 for remainder of the last century. However, with the emergence of industrial economies in China, India, and other developing countries, strong demand and political events have driven crude oil prices as high as almost $140 a barrel.

Jumps in the price of oil have a disruptive effect on the U.S. economy. The increase in the 1970s helped fuel strong inflation. The high price of crude oil translated to dramatic price increases in gasoline, which affected consumers by leaving reduced amounts for expenditures on other items. Consumers showed a greater tendency for smaller cars that were more fuel efficient, which opened the U.S. door to foreign automobile manufacturers. The crude oil price increase in the last decade has brought a change in consumer preferences for hybrid and electric vehicles.

Oil price and gasoline price data are widely available on the Internet. One public source of price data is the Energy Information Administration (EIA) of the U.S. Department of Energy.[11] The EIA provides prices of crude oil on a daily, weekly, monthly, quarterly, and annual basis.

Crude oil prices vary considerably depending on the quality of the oil and where it is drilled and delivered. One popular reference price is the spot price of West Texas Intermediate (WTI) light sweet crude oil delivered to Cushing, Oklahoma and exchanged on the New York Mercantile Exchange. A second popular reference price is the spot price of Brent European North Sea crude oil. These two spot prices tend to move in tandem, but sometimes there are discrepancies caused by excess supplies. Both prices are reported by the EIA and other financial websites and media.

Agricultural Prices

One of the oldest programs in data collection in the United States is in the study of its agricultural sector. While the United States became the largest industrial economy in the world during the twentieth century, the country expanded geographically in the nineteenth century, and agriculture was usually the first major means of livelihood in newly settled territories.

Most working Americans at the time were farmers and ranchers. When small farmers began to struggle in the early twentieth century as the result of intense competition and risk from climate, price support programs were created to stabilize the farming economy, supported by a substantial data collection operation by the U.S. Department of Agriculture.

The National Agriculture Statistics Service (NASS) issues a report near the conclusion of every month that reports on agricultural prices in that month.[12] The report lists prices received for a wide range of crops and livestock, as well as prices paid by farmers for resources. Collective indexes for prices received and prices paid are provided as well, currently using the three-year period of 1990–1992 as the base period.

The prices received index is considered a leading indicator of food-related items in the PPI and CPI. Fuel is a significant input to crop production, so dramatic changes in fuel costs will drive changes in crop prices received. Livestock operations use crops as a feed source, so a price jump in major feed crops like corn will usually result in a price jump for livestock like hogs, cattle, and chickens. In recent decades, corn has been harvested for the production of ethanol, encouraged by government subsidies. This additional consumption has created excess demand for corn, which in turn has driven food prices higher.

CHAPTER 6

Indicators of Interest Rates

Many transactions in the economy would not occur if the buyer needed to have funds readily available to use as payment. Most households would not be able to purchase homes without borrowing a portion of the purchase price. Some financially constrained households would not be able to meet daily living needs without the ability to borrow. Other households have excess funds that are not needed immediately and may place those funds in bank accounts or bonds to be used as a source of loans to others, in exchange for earning a return on their money.

New businesses are usually unable to establish a credible operation without loans, and existing businesses may need to borrow to pursue potentially advantageous expansion. Even when individuals and businesses have assets available, those assets may not be readily liquid or the parties prefer to borrow to meet expenses because the cost to borrow is less than the return they expect to gain from investing their assets elsewhere. Additionally, firms may experience delays in receipt of revenues that preclude the timely payment of expenditures and need a short-term loan to bridge the gap.

Governments are also borrowers. In the U.S. federal government, borrowing was largely limited to times of war in the first 150 years of its history. However, after the Great Depression, the federal government engaged in borrowing to create social programs, execute public projects like the Interstate Highway System, and hire or support unemployed individuals, allowing its total expenditures to exceed revenues. Even for governments that operate with balanced budgets, expenditures may occur sooner than the revenues arrive to cover them, and governments need to do short-term borrowing until the revenues arrive. For example, the federal government operates on a fiscal year of October to September. Federal expenditures are relatively even throughout the year, but a large portion of its revenue comes from annual income taxes filed in April.

The U.S. economic system is often called a capitalist system, which indicates the central role of capital in the basic functioning of the system. Companies need to raise capital by either enlisting investors or borrowing money. Consequently, financial institutions play a key role in the success of the overall economy by creating markets for borrowing.

While a loan differs from most goods or services in the sense that the funds are returned to the party that provided the loan, there is a price paid for the gained opportunity for the borrower and the lost opportunity of the loaning party in the temporary use of the funds. Interest rates are the prices charged for loans. When a loan is negotiated, the interest rate must be sufficiently high for the creditor and sufficiently low for the borrower. Because there are many borrowers and many with funds to loan, parties can shop for the most favorable rate. Just as market prices for goods move toward an equilibrium that balances supply and demand, interest rates move toward an equilibrium that balances amounts creditors provide and borrowers seek.

There are many types of loans and interest rates vary according to the type of loan and borrower. Loans can range in duration from very short, say overnight, to very long, even decades. Some loans are secured by assets that the creditor has rights to if the borrower defaults, while other loans are not secured. Some borrowers are more "credit-worthy" than others in the sense that there is a higher likelihood they will have funds to make repayments of principal and interest. Some loans are repaid with interest all at once, some have periodic interest payments but all principal paid at once, and others (like mortgages) have periodic payments of both principal and interest.

Interest rates are also affected by the state of the economy. Since inflation causes money to lose purchasing power, interest rates generally include a component to compensate the creditor for the lost value caused by expected inflation. Since interest rates are the collective result of decisions by many individuals and institutions, changes in interest rates can serve as a barometer of sentiment about future inflation and the direction of the general economy. Interest rates move to create a balance between loaning and borrowing, so when the economy is more active there is greater demand for borrowing and interest rates move upward.

Tax laws require some interest receipts be considered taxable income, while other types of interest receipts are not; if a creditor expects to pay tax on the interest, the interest rate will generally be higher. Borrowing crosses national borders, with the United States being a significant net borrower from other nations, so interest rates in the United States are affected by interest rates outside the United States.

This chapter will cover several key interest rates that are reported regularly in the business media and can change on a daily basis. Interest rates for other kinds of loans are often closely tied to one of these key rates and therefore the key rates discussed here serve as proxies for other similar loans.

Federal Funds Rate

In order to prevent banks from overextending and to maintain the confidence of the bank's depositors, U.S. banks are required to have on hand an amount in overnight reserves of at least a stated fraction of the total balances of their depositors. If banks are loaning out an amount that reduces those reserves below the specified limit, they can borrow overnight for the sole purpose of meeting reserve requirements.[1]

One source of overnight loans is other banks. Since the borrowing bank will have multiple options, the overnight rate charged is somewhat competitive and works toward an equilibrium value called the *federal funds rate*. Since banks also attract funds from deposits in checking and savings accounts, there is a relationship between the federal funds rate and interest rates offered to depositors. Thus, the movement in the federal funds rate is a reasonable proxy for other short-term interest rates on bank deposits and in money market mutual funds.

The federal funds interest rate is strongly influenced by actions of the Federal Reserve. As part of its mission, the Federal Reserve buys and sells a large quantity of U.S. government debt. Its sizeable presence in the market for this debt alters the effective interest rate earned by buyers of those debt instruments. In fact, the Federal Reserve actually sets a target rate for the federal funds rate and executes purchases and sales of debt to keep the actual rate that banks charge each other for overnight loans close to that rate. The target rate had been a single value to be maintained until adjusted. In recent years, the Fed has announced a range in which it will try to keep the effective federal funds rate.

The Federal Reserve also acts as source of overnight loans to financial institutions. The *discount rate* posted by the Federal Reserve is the financial charge for these loans. The Federal Reserve actually has multiple discount rates depending on the borrower. The lowest discount rate is for primary credit, which would be offered to major banks. For many years, this discount rate was widely reported as the key short-term interest rate set by the Federal Reserve. However, most overnight loans are made between banks, and the effective federal funds rate (the rate actually charged, not the target) is now the major rate reported in the business media.

Figure 6.1 shows the effective federal funds rate (monthly average) from 1955 to 2010. The rate was low in the 1950s, but then climbed in the 1960s and 1970s due to inflationary pressures in the U.S. economy and increasing deficit spending by the federal government. As a means of breaking the high inflation rate in the late 1970s, the Federal Reserve, under the leadership of chairman Paul Volcker, intentionally pushed the federal funds target and discount rates higher to break the inflationary cycle. The strategy was successful, with inflation rates dropping significantly in just a few years. The federal funds rate has gradually declined since the 1980s. In the response to crises in financial markets in 2002 and again in 2008, the Federal Reserve dropped the target rate to near zero.

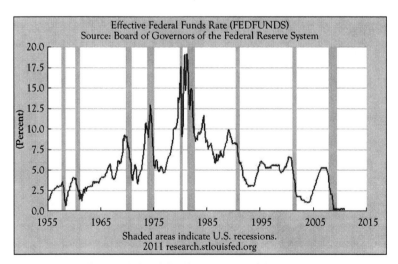

Figure 6.1. Effective federal funds rate, monthly average from 1955 to 2010. (Source: Federal Reserve Bank of St. Louis, FRED Economic Data.)

The Prime Rate

Banks cover their expenses and earn profit by making loans at higher interest rates than they pay to borrow money from depositors and other sources. The rate charged on loans from banks and other bank-like institutions, like credit unions, varies based on the length of the loan and credit-worthiness of the borrower. Less credit-worthy borrowers pay a higher interest rate because there is increased risk that these borrowers may become delinquent in repayment of principal and interest, potentially even defaulting on the loans.

Normally longer-term loans have a higher interest rate because the bank protects itself from the potential of higher interest rates that it may need to pay depositors and creditors in the future. However, this is not always the case, especially in periods like recessions when depositors and creditors have less cash to offer.

The *prime rate* is the interest rate that major banks charge their customers who have the lowest risk of delinquency or default for short-term loans. These low-risk clients are typically blue-chip corporations with stable revenue streams. Although these loans are technically negotiated between a bank and a borrower, since large borrowers can move freely between banks without being constrained by geography, and banks can likewise approve only the loans that pay the best interest rate, the rate that major banks charge these credit-worthy clients quickly converges to a similar competitive interest rate. This common rate is widely available in business print and Internet media sites.

Figure 6.2 displays the average monthly prime rate from 1955 to 2010. Note that the prime rate has a similar pattern to the effective federal funds rate, but is generally higher at any given time. Typically the prime rate runs about 3% above the federal funds rate, although this spread may vary depending on the health of corporate earnings.

Treasury Debt Rates

The U.S. Department of the Treasury manages an enormous amount of borrowing on behalf of the nation. Some of the borrowing is short-term to compensate for differences in timing between revenues and expenditures.

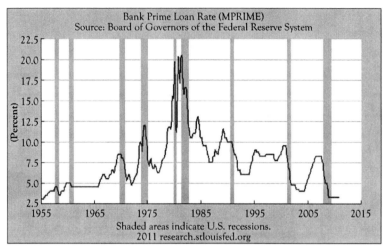

Figure 6.2. U.S. bank prime rate, monthly average, from 1955 to 2010. (Source: Federal Reserve Bank of St. Louis, FRED Economic Data.)

However, much of the borrowing is due to budget deficits. After many years of growing deficits, the United States has a massive sustaining debt that exceeded 14 trillion dollars at the end of the 2010 and caused political havoc in Washington, D.C. over the summer of 2011. This debt is supported by longer term borrowing and refinanced loans when those instruments come due.

The United States borrows via a number of different instruments: Treasury bills, Treasury notes, Treasury bonds, Treasury Inflation-Protected Securities (TIPS), and savings bonds. Treasury bills are the debt with the shortest maturities, mostly 4 weeks, 13 weeks, 26 weeks, or 52 weeks. Treasury notes have intermediate terms of 2, 3, 5, 7, and 10 years. Treasury bonds have 20- or 30-year maturities. All of these instruments have fixed interest rates.

TIPS are notes and bonds that adjust the principal for inflation (based on the CPI-U consumer price index) and pay interest at a stated rate based on the inflation-adjusted principal. These are available with 5-, 10-, and 30-year terms.

Savings bonds are instruments that pay back principal plus interest at redemption. Savings bonds earn interest for up to 30 years, but can be redeemed after 5 years without penalty. EE Savings Bonds pay at a fixed rate of interest, while I Savings Bonds pay at a variable rate of interest based on the CPI-U index.

Interest rates for Treasury bills, notes, bonds, and TIPS are determined by auctions. Auctions are tentatively scheduled and then formally announced shortly before the actual auction takes place. Savings bond rates are set by the Treasury and are really oriented for individual savers. Details of how auctions are conducted are available on the Treasury Department's TreasuryDirect website.[2]

The original purchase of Treasury debt via auctions is called the primary market. Since the actual price of the debt is based on the settlement price of the auction, the effective interest rate earned, called the *yield*, may differ from the stated interest rate. However, Treasury debt instruments, especially notes and bonds, are frequently resold on the secondary market. Due to changes in bond prices, even when interest payments are fixed, yields may change during the life of the Treasury debt instrument.

While Treasury auctions occur frequently and yields from auction settlements are announced, the key tracking indicator of the rate of interest earned on Treasury debt instruments is the yield on the secondary market. Figure 6.3 shows the average monthly yield on 13-week Treasury bills

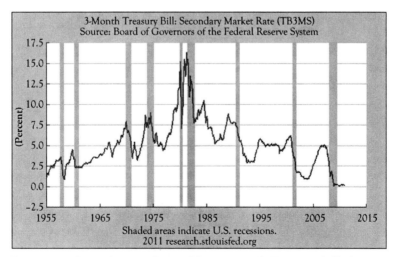

Figure 6.3. Secondary market yield on 13-week Treasury bills from 1955 to 2010. (Source: Federal Reserve Bank of St. Louis, FRED Economic Data.)

from 1955 through 2010. This rate very closely tracks the effective federal funds rate.

Figure 6.4 shows the average monthly effective interest rate on 10-year Treasury notes. For many years, the 30-year Treasury bond represented rates on Treasury debt with longer maturities. However, in the 1990s, during which the United States ran at a surplus for a few years, the Treasury discontinued the 30-year bond for a period of time (although it has now been restarted.) The 10-year note became the reference long-term instrument. Notice that the rates are more stable and tend to zigzag less than the Treasury bill yield in Figure 6.3. The 10-year yield tends to be a little higher than the Treasury bill rate, particularly when rates are low. However, there are months when short-term yields exceed yields on Federal debt with longer maturities.

Effective interest rates on the range of maturities are frequently depicted graphically on a *yield curve*. Figure 6.5 shows an example of a yield curve for treasury debt. Normally the curve will move upward for longer maturities. When the climb in the yield curve is greater, the curve suggests that money is readily available for short-term needs, and the higher rates on long-term maturities are due to higher borrowing

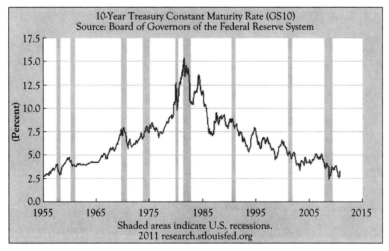

Figure 6.4. Monthly yield on 10-year Treasury notes from 1955 to 2010. (Source: Federal Reserve Bank of St. Louis, FRED Economic Data.)

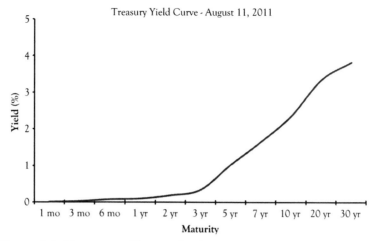

Treasury Yield Curve - August 11, 2011

Figure 6.5. Treasury yield curve for August 11, 2011. (Data source: U.S. Treasury Department.)

demand from businesses looking to expand. There are times when the yield curve drops as the maturities increase, which is known as an inverted yield curve. This typically occurs when money is tight in the economy, and there is diminished demand for debt to fund growth in the economy. Inverted curves often precede a recession.

Since the comparison of Treasury debt rates reflects demands for different kinds of borrowing, the pattern of yields can be a leading indicator for economic activity. The difference between the yield on 10-year Treasury notes and the effective federal funds rate is a component of the Leading Economic Index. An increase in the 10-year rate minus the federal funds rate typically indicates expansion of the economy.

Other Bond Rates

Rates on Treasury debt are widely used as indicators of interest rates because these instruments are sold in large volumes and the market rates are fairly stable. Since parties with funds to loan have a choice between Treasuries and other debt instruments, the interest rates of other debt tends to move in tandem with treasury rates on debt of similar maturity.

One important class of other interest-bearing debt instruments is corporate bonds. Firms require capital for expanding operations as well as meeting short-term operating needs. Some of that capital is provided in the form of equity ownership, but the owners often borrow some of that capital so they do not need to share the profits with other equity owners and make a higher return on the equity they have invested.

Corporate bond rates are typically higher than Treasury debt of a similar maturity because the U.S. Government is viewed as having very low risk of default. Corporate bonds themselves vary considerably based on the risk level. Corporate bonds with low risk are called investment grade bonds and usually are sold initially by large blue-chip corporations. More risky corporate bonds are called high yield or "junk" bonds and are used by smaller firms, as well as by larger firms with questionable prospects for being profitable enough to pay bond interest. Typical corporate bond yields for different grades of bonds are posted in business media and on financial websites.

Another major category of bonds are municipal bonds issued by state and local governments for financing long-term projects and covering short-term cash needs. Although any single issue of a municipal bond is probably more risky than a Treasury debt instrument, interest on municipal bonds receives favorable tax-free treatment by the IRS and makes this debt more favorable at lower rates. Further, investors can reduce the higher risk of municipal bonds by diversifying their holdings of these instruments. Some financial websites report typical municipal bond yields for different maturities.[3]

Mortgage Rates

Over 60% of American households own their own home. Government policy has supported home ownership with deductibility of mortgage interest and backing the credit of agencies that finance home mortgages. Home mortgages are the dominant source of debt for households, and mortgage payments constitute a large fraction of monthly household expenses. Mortgage rates have a significant effect on the size of these payments and are watched carefully by consumers, financial institutions, and public policy officials.

There are different types of mortgages. Two key factors are the length of the mortgage and whether the interest rate is fixed or variable.

Figure 6.6. Average monthly conventional 30-year mortgage rates from 1972 to 2010. (Source: Federal Reserve Bank of St. Louis, FRED Economic Data.)

Many mortgages have maturities of 15 and 30 years, with 15-year mortgages usually having slightly lower interest rates. Figure 6.6 shows the average interest rates on new 30-year conventional fixed-rate mortgages. Mortgage rates have followed a pattern similar to other long-term debt. Mortgage rates approached 20% in the early 1980s when the Federal Reserve was pushing interest rates high to break inflation. Since then, mortgage rates have steadily dropped for the same reasons as other interest rates have dropped, with the 30-year rate below 5% for the first time in decades.

When mortgage rates climbed in the 1970s and 1980s, lending institutions began offering variable rate loans to offer the borrower an opportunity to start the mortgage at a lower interest rate, but with a capability to increase interest rates and adjust monthly payments if market bond rates increased, to protect the party making the loan. Many of these loans peg the adjustments to the variable mortgage rate to the Cost of Funds Index (COFI). This is an index prepared by the Federal Home Loan Bank of San Francisco that is determined by the ratio of interest expenses to total funds of member institutions in the district of the San Francisco Bank.[4]

Consumer Credit Rates

In addition to borrowing to buy a home, many consumers also borrow money for major purchases such as a new car, new appliance, or to cover other living, educational, or maintenance expenses. Banks and savings institutions set loan rates for new car purchases. Automobile manufacturers also have financing divisions that make loans on new car purchases and are generally a little lower than commercial banks.

Banks also make personal loans to consumers, often as part of a credit card plan. Some retailers like department stores and gasoline companies issue their own credit cards or have lines of credit. These rates are typically much higher when the loan is not secured by property, due to increased risk of nonpayment. The Federal Reserve releases a quarterly report with average rates for automobile and personal loans in the middle month of the quarter.[5] The release is usually scheduled around the fifth day of the month, with a preliminary report in the second month after the quarter ends and a revised report the following month.

Banks offer home equity loans that allow consumers to borrow money using their home as collateral, either for home improvement or for other financial needs. Banks also offer home equity lines of credit that are pre-approved loans using the home to secure the loan. Typical interest rates charged on these loans are listed on the website bankrate.com.[6]

CHAPTER 7

Indicators of Resource Utilization

In order for the economy to provide the goods and services desired by households and needed by industry and government, capacity must be available to produce those goods and services. This capacity comes in the form of a labor force, plants and buildings, and equipment. When capacity is nearly fully utilized, some demand will be unmet and may result in inflationary pressures as firms outbid other firms for these resources. When productive resources are used well below capacity, the incomes of resource providers will suffer and result in contractionary pressures on economic activity. This chapter focuses on economic indicators that measure the utilization of productive resources.

The Unemployment Rate

Along with the GDP and the CPI, the unemployment rate is among the most widely reported economic indicators. Since it deals with an issue that directly affects the welfare of households, the level of unemployment concerns the general public and has a strong impact on political discourse. As we will discuss in chapter 9, unemployment is a key issue in macroeconomic policy.

The main report on U.S. unemployment is assembled and issued by the Bureau of Labor Statistics in the Department of Labor. The report and statistical indicators are based on household surveys conducted as part of the Current Population Survey, which assesses the situation in the household on the 12th day of the month. Initial estimates of unemployment are reported on the first Friday of the following month in a report entitled *The Employment Situation*, with revisions in later monthly reports.[1]

The unemployment rate is based on a definition of an unemployed person as someone of working age who does not have a job and who has attempted to find a job in the past four weeks. This definition includes persons who are receiving unemployment benefits and individuals who are not. The report provides separate unemployment rates for different demographic subpopulations: by gender, ethnicity, age group, and education.

There are individuals who are not working, but who are not counted in the calculation of the unemployment rate. One group, called 'discouraged' workers, are not working, want to work, but are not seeking work as actively as in the above definition of unemployed. Another group, called 'marginally attached to the labor force,' consists of people who are not working for noneconomic reasons, but who want to eventually return to the labor force. Also, there are individuals who are employed part-time, some of whom are prevented from working more either due to economic factors (these people are sometimes called 'underemployed') or for personal, noneconomic reasons. The monthly report provides estimates of the number of people in these categories.

Employment is strongly affected by the calendar, with many jobs created for a portion of the year due to climate (for example, construction, agriculture, and sports) and holidays (for example, retail and education). Consequently, unemployment rates are seasonally adjusted for most reports to distinguish changes in unemployment rates associated with the business cycle from changes that typically occur at that time of the year.

Figure 7.1 displays the monthly unemployment rate from 1960 to 2010. The graph shows that the unemployment rate spikes upward sharply during recessions, then declines at a slower rate after recessions. Although the unemployment rate moves primarily with business cycles, the graph indicates a slow upward trend over the 50-year period. One explanation for this upward movement is the phenomenon of *structural unemployment*, whereby there is an increased tendency of a mismatch of the skills demanded by employers with those who are looking for work. With technological change occurring at a faster pace, workers no longer can rely on a skill set to carry them through an entire career and may need retraining after their prior occupation is no longer in demand.

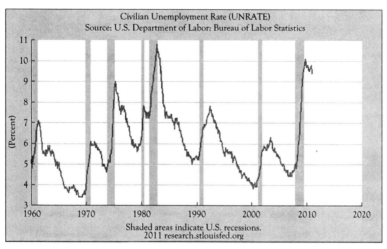

Figure 7.1. U.S. civilian unemployment rate, monthly and seasonally adjusted, from 1960 to 2010. (Source: Federal Reserve Bank of St. Louis, FRED Economic Data.)

Technological change has also resulted in replacing human labor with automation, with replacements for those lost jobs dependent on the creation of new jobs and industries for which displaced workers can be trained.

The unemployment rate is inversely related to growth in real GDP, a relationship formalized as *Okun's Law*. There is also a clear and observable inverse relationship between the unemployment rate and inflation. This relationship can be explained by more intense competition for labor services when unemployment is low, but weakened demand and softening price pressures when unemployment is high. The graphical relationship between unemployment rate and inflation rate is known as the *Phillips curve*.

In a society where there is a strong sentiment that one's right to consume is conditional on one's willingness to work and pay one's way, the ideal economy may seem to be one where everyone who wants to work can find a suitable job. However, most economists contend the economy is better off when the unemployment rate is higher than zero due to the inflationary pressures of low unemployment and inevitable structural unemployment. While there is no consensus on what the ideal level is, most assessments would be an unemployment rate of at least 4%.

Initial Unemployment Insurance Claims

When employees lose their jobs involuntarily, under certain conditions they can file for unemployment insurance benefits with the state where they reside. Since the initial filing for these benefits will normally occur near the beginning of a period of unemployment, data on the number of filings can provide an advance indication of when unemployment is on the rise or decline.

The Employment and Training Administration of the U.S. Department of Labor gathers data from states on the number of initial claims for unemployment insurance that are filed during a week and prepares a report issued the following Thursday.[2] The number of new claims is reported seasonally adjusted and unadjusted. Because the timing of the number of new claims is subject to random fluctuation and large employee layoffs can cause the claims to occur unevenly, the report includes a seasonally adjusted four-week moving average of initial unemployment insurance claims.

Figure 7.2 is a graph of the seasonally adjusted four-week moving average of initial unemployment insurance claims from 1970 to 2010. The pattern of the time series in the graph resembles that in the graph of

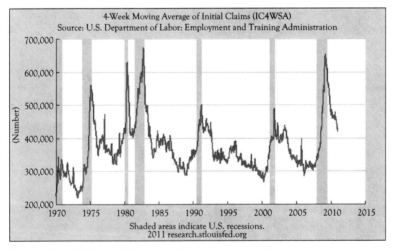

Figure 7.2. U.S. initial unemployment claims, four-week moving average and seasonally adjusted, from 1970 to 2010. (Source: Federal Reserve Bank of St. Louis, FRED Economic Data.)

the unemployment rate in Figure 7.1. The figure also indicates that the number of initial claims usually begins to increase steadily in advance of a recession. As noted in chapter 3, this is one of the components of the Leading Economic Index. And since the report of new claims is issued weekly, rather than monthly or quarterly, this indicator gives more immediate feedback on the health of the economy.

The Monster Employment Index

The Internet has become the primary venue for job announcements, job searching, and even job applications. The online employment website Monster.com created an index in 2004 to track online job posting activity.[3] The monthly report is issued at the beginning of the month, usually one day prior to the Labor Department's employment report.

The main indicator is a national index with base value of 100, using 2003 as the base period. The index climbed to above 180 in 2007, but decreased during the recession, although remaining above 100, meaning there continued to be more job openings posted on Monster.com during the recession than in 2003. The Monster.com report includes indexes for components of the job search listings, broken down by type of job, by region of the nation, and for several major cities.

This indicator reflects an upward trend, particularly in the past when the general population migrated toward use of the Internet. Still, the breadth and relevance of the data makes the index of interest and the upward trend caused by an increased awareness of online postings will likely diminish in the future.

Average Workweek

The rate of unemployment is a partial indication of how well the labor force is being employed. Another factor is how many hours per week workers are typically employed. The Bureau of Labor Statistics conducts regular surveys of firms as part of its Establishment Survey, which includes gathering information to estimate the average number of hours worked per week. The report is included as part of the monthly report, *The Employment Situation*, released the first Friday of the month.[4]

The main indicator of average hours worked per week currently applies to all employees on private nonfarm payrolls. This measure recently expanded from a measure of average hours worked per week for production and nonsupervisory employees on nonfarm payrolls. The two measures are usually similar, however.

Figure 7.3 displays the time series that applies to all production and nonsupervisory employees on nonfarm payrolls from 1965 to 2010. While there are clear drops in the measure during the intervals corresponding to recessions, the dominant change is the downward trend from nearly 39 hours per week to between 33 and 34 hours per week.

The monthly report of average workweeks includes estimates for different groups of industries in the private sector. Not all industries show the same pattern as Figure 7.3. Figure 7.4 shows the average weekly hours for manufacturing firms. For this indicator, average hours per week are not declining over time. In fact, when the economy is healthy, the average exceeds 40 hours a month, reflecting overtime. For these industries, firms use overtime to meet increases in demand and then scale back overtime when demand drops and finally cut back some workers to part-time. The manufacturing average work hours also start to

Figure 7.3. Average weekly hours for U.S. production and nonsupervisory workers in private industry, seasonally adjusted, from 1965 to 2010. (Source: Federal Reserve Bank of St. Louis, FRED Economic Data.)

Figure 7.4. Average weekly hours for U.S. production and nonsupervisory workers in manufacturing, seasonally adjusted, from 1965 to 2010. (Source: Federal Reserve Bank of St. Louis, FRED Economic Data.)

drop ahead of a recession as managers start seeing reductions in orders and decide to cut production before inventories grow too much. For this reason, the average workweek for manufacturing is included as a component in the Leading Economic Index.

Productivity

In order for working Americans to be able to increase their consumption and standard of living, either more resources (labor, capital, land) are needed or businesses and government need to discover ways to get more output out of the resource inputs available. The expansion of productive resources is limited. Most available land that is suitable for productive uses is already in use. Capital is also in limited supply and increasingly sought outside the United States. And while in times of recession, many Americans would like the opportunity to work or work more, at some point working significantly more hours detracts from the standard of living.

The alternative of getting more output out of productive resources has been successful in the United States and the world. This occurs by increasing the skills of workers through education and training, developing more effective and efficient machinery, better management, and discovering and applying knowledge to create new technologies and reduce waste of resources.

There are measures of *productivity* that assess the ratio of units of output generated to units of input applied. Since labor is a key productive resource (over 50% of the resource cost of the GDP) and wage and salary levels are roughly tied to the marginal revenue gained by their activity, one key measure of productivity is the ratio between the output of the economy, or sector of the economy, and the number of labor hours used to create that output.

The Bureau of Labor Statistics compiles a report, called *Productivity and Costs*, which estimates labor productivity on a quarterly basis.[5] The calculated ratio is the portion of GDP that is provided by the private business sector in real dollars for a quarter, divided by the total number of labor-hours applied during the quarter. A preliminary report is issued early in the second month after the featured quarter ends, with a revised report early in the next month. This ratio is converted to an index with base year of 2005. Each quarter's productivity is also expressed in terms of the percent increase from the last quarter and from the same quarter a year earlier. The calculations are seasonally adjusted.

Figure 7.5 shows the change in the index of labor productivity from 1950 to 2010. There has been a steady increase in labor productivity, more than tripling over the 60-year period in the figure. It is interesting to note that productivity does not always languish during a recession. In fact, as shown in the areas designated by gray bars on the graph, productivity rose sharply during the last two recessions. This is probably explained by pressures on the workers who retained their jobs to work harder and more efficiently to keep themselves in jobs and their employers in business.

The increase in labor productivity over the last 60 years has been driven in good part by the increased effectiveness of capital, in the form of more powerful machines, computers, and better materials. Due to increased automation, capital has replaced what had been done by labor and also made the labor more effective. The BLS calculates a measure of productivity relative to the combination of labor and capital, called *multifactor productivity*. A preliminary annual report is provided in May

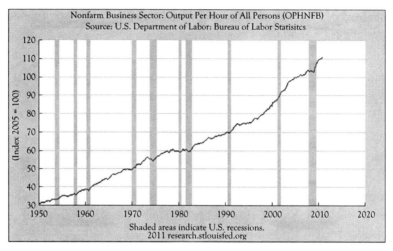

Figure 7.5. Index of U.S. labor productivity from 1950 to 2010, base year 2005. (Source: Federal Reserve Bank of St. Louis, FRED Economic Data.)

of the following year, with revised and more detailed reports later in the fall.[6] This productivity measure is a ratio of GDP output to the combined amount of labor and capital, using a chain-type index to reflect changes in the mix of labor and capital over time. Separate measurements of labor productivity gains relative to shifts in the composition of labor and relative to increased capital intensity appear in the report.

In their May 19, 2011 news release, the BLS reported that between 1987 and 2010, multifactor productivity increased at a compound annual rate of 1.0% per year, while overall labor productivity increased at a compound annual rate of 2.3% per year.[7] During that period, labor inputs increased by only 1.1%, while services due to capital resources increased by 3.7%. Hence, much of the impressive growth in labor productivity is due to application of capital. Interestingly, the productivity per dollar of input of capital services actually diminished at a compound annual rate of 0.8% during the period.

Capacity Utilization

Just as the labor force of the country or a region may be underutilized in the sense that there are people willing to work or work more, unused productive capacity can exist in other forms: plants that are idle or running partial shifts, equipment and machinery that are idle more than expected for normal use, and commercial transportation vehicles that are idle or partly empty. Idle capacity is inevitable in recessions when operations are suspended due to the lack of demand. However, some capacity may be idle even when the economy is healthy and near an expansion peak, due to changes in the demands for goods and services or as a consequence of excessive capacity expansion.

The Federal Reserve assembles data to estimate what fraction of capacity is utilized, as part of its monthly report on industrial production,[8] which includes values for the Industrial Production Index described in chapter 3. Managers of surveyed private businesses report how much output they produced during a month and estimate how much output would be reasonably possible if all equipment and machinery operated at normal capacity and were properly staffed by labor.

Figure 7.6 shows capacity utilization from 1970 to 2010. The graph indicates that capacity utilization drops sharply as the economy enters recession, and then almost immediately begins to recover when the recession ends, although the recovery in the capacity utilization rate is slower

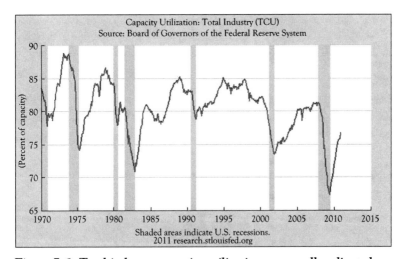

Figure 7.6. Total industry capacity utilization, seasonally adjusted, from 1970 to 2010. (Source: Federal Reserve Bank of St. Louis, FRED Economic Data.)

than the decline and sometimes sputters even when the economy does not officially go into recession.

Earlier in the chapter, we mentioned that economists do not regard an economy with no unemployment as a feasible, or even a desirable, goal. Along with some unemployment caused by workers displaced from one job while seeking another, low unemployment can result in inflationary pressures if employers must compete aggressively for the services of workers. Similarly, if nearly all productive capacity is in use, new products or expansion of existing products can only happen by outbidding and displacing the other production activities using the plants and equipment. Economists generally regard a capacity utilization rate of 85% as being high enough to trigger inflation.

As is evident in Figure 7.6, despite the dominant impact of business cycles on capacity utilization, capacity utilization has been trending downward. The measure barely topped 80% just prior to the last recession and dropped lower than in prior recessions. Perhaps changes in the structure of the economy, such as the shift of domestic production to foreign locations or the 'greening' of the economy, are resulting in more idle capacity.

Business Inventories

In order to respond to demand, sellers need to have some materials, parts, and finished goods on hand. If a retailer does not have a good in stock when a customer wants to make a purchase, the customer may not be willing to wait, and the retailer may lose the sale. If a wholesale supplier does not have goods in stock when retailers need to replenish their stock, the retailer may find another supplier. Likewise, manufacturers need to be able to meet demand from their clients in a timely manner by having parts and raw materials in ready supply.

At the same time, inventories tie up resources of a business, whether it is financial capital or expenditure on labor, raw materials, and other production costs. Excessive inventories or items that remain in inventory for a long time not only add costs, but also indicate some inefficiency in the general economy.

Viewed from the perspective of the economy, inventories should rise when the rate of economic activity increases to keep the activity flowing, but be scaled back when the economy contracts. However, due to the uncertainty of the change in activity, firms may underestimate economic expansions and inventories may be drawn down to low levels. Low inventories in an expanding economy can stir price inflation. On the other hand, when the economy contracts, some firms may be caught by surprise and inventories rise significantly. High levels of inventory can cause firms to scale back production to liquidate inventory, resulting in employee layoffs and scaled back purchases from their suppliers. These actions encourage more economic contraction.

The Census Bureau tracks inventory levels on a monthly basis in its *Manufacturing and Trade Inventories and Sales* report.[9] The report is based on surveys of manufacturers, wholesale dealers, and retailers. The manufacturers' inventory estimate includes materials and in process goods, as well as finished goods. The report is issued the middle of the second month following the month featured in the report and includes estimates of inventory levels and changes in inventory levels. The estimates are adjusted for typical seasonal variation and trading days in the month.

Business inventories generally increase due to the increase in the GDP, although the value typically decreases toward the conclusion of recessions. Another useful indicator of the status of inventories is to look at the ratio of inventory to sales in the month. Figure 7.7 shows this ratio for months

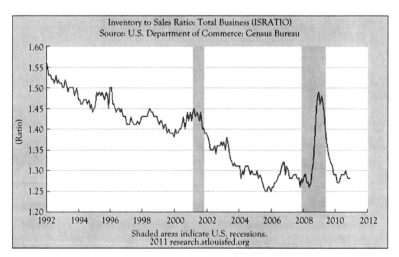

Figure 7.7. Total industry inventory to sales ratio, seasonally adjusted, from 1992 to 2010. (Source: Federal Reserve Bank of St. Louis, FRED Economic Data.)

in 1992 through 2010. One interesting facet of this graph is that the ratio jumped dramatically in the recession that began in late 2007, but did not show a similar pattern in the recession of 2001. This likely occurred because the recession in 2001 was less severe and did not result in much decrease in household demand.

Another interesting observation about Figure 7.7 is that the ratio declined considerably from 1992 until the depth of the recession in 2008. This decrease may reflect the increased use of computer and communications technology to give more timely notices of downstream purchases to upstream suppliers, allowing firms to operate more effectively with lower inventories. Many firms in supply-chain arrangements even integrate their information systems to track inventory and to time deliveries closer to when the customer needs them.

Crude Oil and Natural Gas Inventories

Crude oil is a critical commodity to the economy, essential to the transportation sector in the form of gasoline and other fuels, as well as needed for other industrial products and processes. As noted in chapter 5, crude oil is subject to dramatic jumps in price, which wreak havoc on the economy and stimulate inflation. Crude oil is especially prone to price increases when stocks of crude oil are low or disasters that limit production or imports threaten to drain inventories, adding uncertainty to the market that suppliers and speculators can exploit.

The Energy Information Administration of the U.S. Department of Energy provides a weekly report about crude oil inventories and many other measures in its *Petroleum Status Report*.[10] The report is available on Wednesdays and reports on activities during the prior week and inventory levels as of the Friday of that week. Crude oil inventories normally vary during the year with higher levels in the summer when there is more automobile use. The EIA report conveys the typical range of inventories to put the current inventory level in perspective.

Another key energy resource for the U.S. economy is natural gas. Natural gas is a widely used household fuel and is an alternative to oil in electricity generation. Natural gas is a more reliable energy source due to large supplies in North America, but if inventories get too low, natural gas prices can jump higher just like oil prices because users of natural gas cannot immediately replace it with alternative fuels.

The EIA publishes a weekly *Natural Gas Storage Report* that monitors natural gas stocks in underground storage.[11] Similar to the petroleum status report, this report compares current stock levels to a typical range for the time of year. Since seasonal variation in natural gas usage is significant, with higher use in the winter for heating, underground storage stocks are typically at their highest in the late fall and at their lowest in the spring.

CHAPTER 8

Indicators of International Exchange

The economic indicators discussed in earlier chapters focused on economic resources, production, and exchanges within the United States. However, even in discussing the composition of the gross domestic product (GDP), we observed that net exports from the United States to locations outside the United States must be recognized to bring consumption of final goods and services into balance with the use of resources to produce final goods and services. Imports add more final goods for domestic use, but draw on the income and wealth within the United States. On the other hand, exports result in more income and wealth coming to the United States, but sacrifice consumption of outputs from domestic productive resources.

Other nations use different currencies and the exchange rates between those currencies and the dollar are subject to change. Currency rate fluctuations may make U.S. exports look more or less expensive to companies abroad and make imports look more or less expensive to domestic companies. Thus, currency exchange rates are a major influence on international trade. Changing exchange rates can affect domestic prices and the inflation rate.

There are also exchanges of financial capital between the United States and the outside world. U.S. residents and businesses invest abroad, and foreign residents and businesses invest in the United States. The U.S. Treasury Department, which is a dominant borrower, allows non-U.S. entities to purchase its debt. These flows of financial capital affect currency exchange rates, the purchasing power of the dollar, and interest rates.

This chapter will focus on indicators that track exchanges, and the environment for exchanges, between the United States and the outside world.

International Trade

Both imports and exports have generally increased over time. This is a natural consequence of growing populations and per capita consumption both in the United States and elsewhere. However, the rate of growth in imports and exports has outpaced the growth in GDP as a result of the increasing internationalization of commerce. When the economy in the U.S. contracts, U.S. imports usually contract as well. Since the United States is a major export destination for other countries, a recession in the United States means a significant drop in other nations' exports, resulting in contractions or recessions in their economies, and in turn those countries import less from the United States. Consequently, U.S. exports often decline in response to a decline in imports.

For much of the early twentieth century, the United States exported more than it imported. This trade surplus resulted from the emergence of the United States as the leading industrial producer and the most productive agricultural country in the world. The United States was also relatively unaffected by the destruction of productive capacity during World Wars I and II. However, with the emergence of other industrialized nations in the latter part of the twentieth century and heavy reliance on imported oil that escalated dramatically in price, the value of U.S. imports grew faster than, and eventually exceeded, the value of its exports.

Import and export activity in goods are monitored by the Census Bureau. The Bureau of Economic Analysis (BEA) tracks imports and exports of services. The BEA reports on the total imports and exports of goods and services monthly, around the second week of the following month.[1] The report has considerable detail, showing the breakdown of imports and exports by type of good or service and by the country with which trade is done.

Petroleum imports and exports are given special attention since petroleum net imports account for about half of the difference between total imports and total exports. For this reason, the reports need to be viewed in the context of trends in petroleum prices.

Figure 8.1 shows total U.S. imports and exports from 1960 to 2010. The higher, thicker line is the graph of total imports, and the lower line represents total exports. Note that both import and export activity drop during recessions, with imports usually declining more than exports.

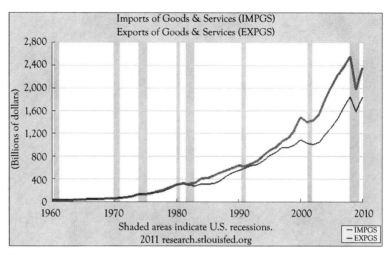

Figure 8.1. Annual U.S. imports (thicker line) and exports from 1960 to 2010. (Source: Federal Reserve Bank of St. Louis, FRED Economic Data.)

Figure 8.1 indicates that while both total imports and exports increased, imports increased faster in general. The difference is called the *trade balance*, which is calculated as the value of exports minus the value of imports, and has been generally negative in recent decades. This negative balance, or trade deficit, grew to about –$750 billion just prior to the recession that began in 2007 but has diminished considerably afterward. Two reasons for the growth in the negative trade balance are (1) the rise in the price of oil in real dollar terms with the United States being a net importer, and (2) the emergence of economies in Asia with cheaper labor and production costs, which has caused domestic production to move offshore. Although the trade imbalance, even at its peak, was just around 6% of GDP, an increasing negative trade balance is a concern to those in charge of macroeconomic policy in the United States, as it results in both an exodus of wealth and a lower demand for domestic resources.

Jumps in exports are regarded as a positive sign for the domestic economy because this generally means increased demand for the dollar worldwide, enhanced domestic economic activity, and more sales and profits for domestic businesses. Jumps in imports relative to jumps in exports can be a sign that foreign prices are lower than domestic prices for the same goods and services, which can put downward pressure on the exchange value of the dollar.

Import and Export Prices

Shifts in imports and exports occur largely due to shifts in prices of imports and exports. The Bureau of Labor Statistics, which collects domestic price data for the CPI and PPI, performs the same task to track changes in import prices and export prices. The BLS manages separate composite indexes for import prices and export prices (with a base year of 2000), published in a monthly report issued near the middle of the month following the month featured in the report.[2] The lead report is usually expressed in terms of percent change from the previous month. The full report provides several supporting indexes for different types of goods, industry groups, and trading partner countries.

Figure 8.2 shows percent changes from a year earlier in the import price index from 1983 to 2010. Figure 8.3 displays percent changes from a year earlier in the export price index from 1984 to 2010. Note the year-to-year changes in these indexes fluctuate much more than domestic inflation rates corresponding to general price indexes like the CPI.

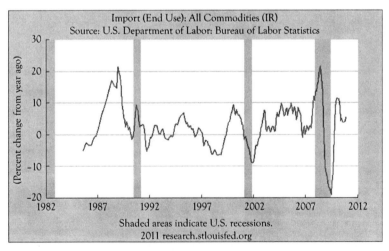

Figure 8.2. Changes in the price index for U.S. imports from one year earlier, not seasonally adjusted, from 1983 to 2010. (Source: Federal Reserve Bank of St. Louis, FRED Economic Data.)

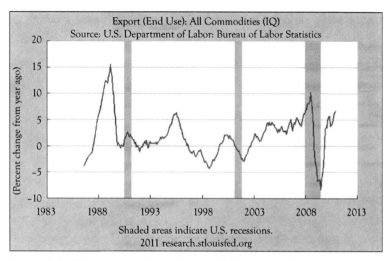

Figure 8.3. Changes in price index for U.S. exports from one year earlier, not seasonally adjusted, from 1984 to 2010. (Source: Federal Reserve Bank of St. Louis, FRED Economic Data.)

A major determinant of the changes in these indexes is the fluctuation of the trade value of the dollar, which affects both import prices and export prices in a similar manner. When the trade value of the dollar goes down, as it did in the 1980s, import and export prices both increase. However, the change in the import price index fluctuates more than the change in the export price index, partly due to fluctuation in oil prices, which have a stronger effect on the import price index.

There is considerable variation in price changes among different types of goods and services, so a change in the overall import or export index does not imply a similar change in the prices of all imported or exported goods and services. In the case of the import price index, petroleum contributes over 25% of the weighting in the index, so a large change in petroleum prices can easily offset price changes in a different direction for a majority of other imported items.

Exchange Rates

Some of the changes in import and export prices are the result of fluctuation in the exchange rates between the dollar and the currencies in the other countries involved in U.S. trade. Since the 1970s, most of the major trading nations now allow their currencies to "float," meaning the exchange rate is determined by currency market mechanisms where participants make bids to buy one currency using another currency, with the settlements establishing the exchange rate. Prior to the early 1970s, exchanges were fixed by negotiation between countries.

Some nations still use fixed exchange rates with the dollar as determined by their central banks. Even in countries that allow their currencies to float, the central banks of those countries may intervene with actions intended to influence currency exchange rates if they deem the exchange rate to be undesirable. If the amount of a foreign currency required to be exchanged for a unit of domestic currency is too high, the country's exports may appear too expensive to foreign buyers. If that exchange rate is too low, the country may have difficulty acquiring sufficient quantities of key imports.

Several factors influence exchange rates. A country that offers higher interest rates will increase the demand for that currency because foreign investors will be willing to give up a larger amount of their currency to acquire that country's currency and deposit money there. Countries with increases in inflation see the exchange rate (in terms of amount of foreign currency per unit of domestic currency) diminish because the purchasing power of their currency is diminishing faster. Countries with negative trade balances face downward pressure on exchange rates because the country will need to use more of its currency, in the net, to make purchases from foreign suppliers. Nations that have high debt or operate at deficits also have downward pressure on exchange rates because they need to attract more creditors, some of whom are foreign. Countries that are growing rapidly or are experiencing faster gains in productivity will tend to see higher exchange rates for their currencies because foreign sources will want to invest there. Political stability is also a positive factor in floating exchange rates since investments in unstable countries have a greater risk of loss.

Currency exchange rates are widely reported in the business media and in real-time on the Internet. Key currencies that float with the dollar include the Canadian dollar, the Mexican peso, the euro, the British pound, the Japanese yen, and the Chinese yuan. The Federal Reserve calculates and announces a weighted index for the value of the dollar relative to other currencies based on the amount of trade associated with each foreign currency.[3] Figure 8.4 shows the monthly average value of the

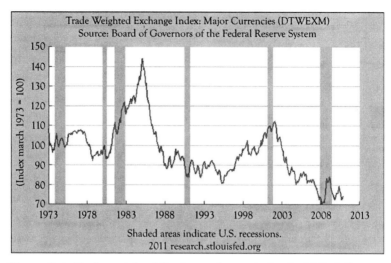

Figure 8.4. Trade-weighted foreign exchange index for U.S. dollar against major currencies, monthly and not seasonally adjusted, from 1973 to 2010. (Source: Federal Reserve Bank of St. Louis, FRED Economic Data.)

exchange rate index for major currencies from 1973 to 2010. The index uses a base month of March 1973. The dollar strengthened to its highest level of this period in the mid-1980s when the United States managed to bring its high inflation of the 1970s under control and the U.S. economy was booming, but then the exchange rate index dropped significantly. The dollar rose in relative value again in the late 1990s, when the United States was running a budget surplus and was at the center of the dot-com boom. However, due to skyrocketing deficits and increasing prices for imported oil, the dollar has declined to now retain roughly 75% of its value relative to other major currencies compared to 1973.

Balance of Payments

When goods and services are exported or imported, payments are received or disbursed by an individual or institution in the United States. However, there are additional transactions that result in funds flowing into or out of the United States: U.S. residents who have investments outside the country receive income in the form of interest or dividends, as do those who reside outside the United States, but receive income from investments within the United States. There are also financial transactions that cross borders when parties in the United States invest capital abroad and vice versa. Another type of cross-border transaction occurs when salaries are paid by U.S. businesses and governments to individuals working abroad, or to foreign nationals within the United States paid from sources abroad.

The net of all these fund transfers over a period is called the *balance of payments*. The BEA gathers data and estimates the balance of payments on quarterly basis in a report called *U.S. International Transactions*.[4] The report is released in the middle of the third month following the end of the quarter.

The balance of payments is divided into three accounts: the current account, the capital account, and the financial account. The current account includes payments related to imports and exports. Thus the trade balances for months within the quarter are part of the current account. The current account also includes income received from abroad or paid from domestic sources to parties abroad in the form of interest, dividends, salaries, pensions, and benefits. Government grants and aid payments are part of the current account as well.

Figure 8.5 shows the seasonally adjusted, quarterly current account balance from 1960 to 2010. The current account balance was close to zero

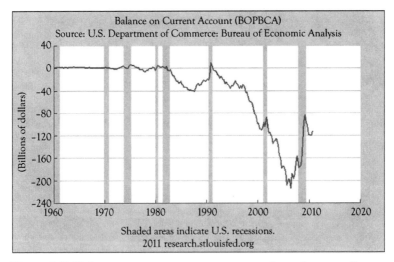

Figure 8.5. Balance on current account, quarterly and seasonally adjusted, from 1960 to 2010. Negative values indicate outflows exceed inflows. (Source: Federal Reserve Bank of St. Louis, FRED Economic Data.)

until the 1980s when the balance in terms of inflows minus outflows went negative. The balance returned to a positive value in the early 1990s, only to drop dramatically until 2006. This deficit balance diminished during the following recession, but has begun to grow again. Changes to the current account balance mirror changes in the trade balance fairly closely, so the negative trend in the current balance largely reflects the increase in imports into the United States and the jump in imported crude oil prices.

The capital account balance is the net value of any transfer of a non-financial asset that is not the result of production activity, either to a U.S. resident, organization, or government entity from a foreign source or to a foreign resident, organization, or government entity from a U.S. source. Transfers to a foreign party would be negative entries. These non-production items include purchases and sales of rights, insurance payments across borders, transfer of assets across borders by immigrants or emigrants, and certain taxes across borders. The capital account balance is usually relatively small compared to the current balance and financial balance.

The financial account aggregates the net amounts from transfers of financial capital by foreign residents and institutions to the United States. Transfers of financial capital by U.S. residents and institutions to foreign locations subtracts from this account balance. For example, a purchase of a Treasury bill by a nonresident would add to the net flow of foreign-owned assets in the United States. A purchase of equity in a foreign company by a U.S. investment bank would increase the flow of U.S. assets abroad, which reduces the financial account balance. Figure 8.6 shows the net flow of foreign assets in the United States and Figure 8.7 shows the net flow of U.S. assets abroad from 1960 to 2010. Note that the values in Figure 8.7 are negative as net flows of U.S. assets abroad offset foreign assets in the United States for balance of payment purposes. Both types of flows increased significantly with time, other than during recessions. The net flows of foreign assets in the United States are generally higher than net flows of U.S. assets abroad, largely to compensate for higher imports than exports in the current account.

In theory, the sum of the balances in the current account, capital account, and financial account should be exactly zero.[5] Any transaction that changes the balance of one of these accounts should be netted out in another. For example, if a U.S. firm exports raw materials, this would contribute

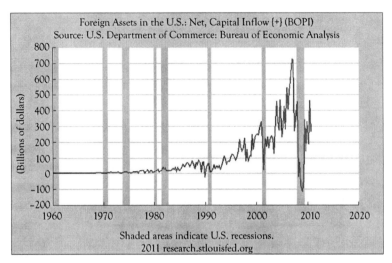

Figure 8.6. Net capital inflow of foreign assets into the U.S., quarterly and seasonally adjusted, from 1960 to 2010. (Source: Federal Reserve Bank of St. Louis, FRED Economic Data.)

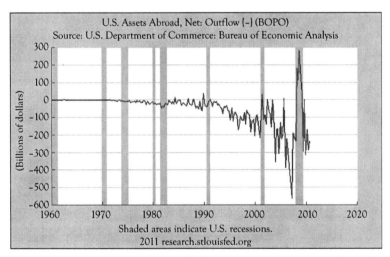

Figure 8.7. Net capital outflow of U.S. assets abroad, quarterly and seasonally adjusted, from 1960 to 2010. (Source: Federal Reserve Bank of St. Louis, FRED Economic Data.)

to increasing the current account by the value of the sale. If the buyer purchased on credit, this would constitute an equivalent increase in the value of U.S. capital held abroad and decrease the financial account. However, the reported account balances are based on data collected for individual accounts, rather than formally done by double-entry accounting. Due to missing items and valuation differences, there are discrepancies that result in a sum of balances different than zero. The seasonal adjustments of the balance can also affect the amount of the discrepancy.

Treasury International Capital

Much of the data used by the BEA to determine the capital account balance in the quarterly balance of payments analysis is collected by the Department of Treasury. A monthly report is prepared showing the net impact of cross-border activity in the purchase and sale of equities, bonds, and short-term debt securities.[6] The report is entitled *Treasury International Capital* and is released around the middle of the second month following the month featured in the report.

The summary measure in the report is the net flow of foreign investments in U.S. financial securities minus U.S. investments of foreign securities. Although this excludes direct investment by companies in overseas affiliates, the Treasury report is monthly and gives more timely feedback on activity in the financial account in the balance of payments, just as the BEA's monthly report on trade provides more timely information on exports and imports in the current account.

International Investment Position

The BEA's *U.S International Transactions* report estimates flows of capital assets across borders. However, U.S. assets held abroad and foreign assets in the United States change in value. Amounts held in corporate equities and commodities change in value with prevailing stock and commodity market prices. Debt instruments change in value due to changes in interest rates. Since these changes in valuations are not considered current income, they are not considered in the balance of payments report.

The BEA publishes an annual report that estimates the total valuation of these assets owned on one side of the U.S. border, but residing or having a liability on the other side of the border. The report is called *International Investment Position* and is released about six months following the year featured in the report.[7] The report states the values, by category, at the end of the year and changes in value for each category from the end of the prior year.

Both foreign assets held in the United States and U.S. assets held abroad have generally increased other than during recessions. Foreign assets in the United States have been about 15% higher than U.S. assets abroad in recent years. This is not necessarily a negative development for the United States, as an exodus of foreign assets would cause disruptions in domestic markets and cause a drop in asset values.

The LIBOR Rate

While other countries have their own currencies, the U.S. dollar is often used as the currency even for transactions outside the United States. Many foreign banks have deposits of *eurodollars* that can be used to facilitate international exchanges. The term "eurodollar" derives from the fact that European banks were the first foreign banks to hold dollars, but eurodollar deposits are held in major foreign banks outside Europe.

The existence of eurodollars provides a convenient medium for international trade. Additionally, eurodollars provide a mechanism for a bank in one country to borrow from banks in other countries in order to meet short-term needs. The British Bankers' Association establishes daily rates for these eurodollar loans, collectively called the London Interbank Offered Rate (LIBOR).[8] One-month, 3-month, 6-month, and 1-year rates are announced each day.

LIBOR rates are the basis for other financial transactions, such as futures contracts and interest rate swaps that allow parties to insure against the risk of changes in exchange rates and interest rates. The LIBOR is also the basis for recalculating rates in some adjustable rate mortgages in the United States.

When the U.S. economy and international financial markets are fairly stable, the LIBOR rate is generally slightly higher than the comparable rate for the Treasury bill of the same duration. This difference is called the "TED spread." The reason the LIBOR is slightly higher is the additional risk that the loan is not backed by the "full faith and credit" of the U.S. Government like Treasury bills. However, when international markets are nervous about the U.S. economy, especially its monetary policy, the TED spread can grow considerably because those who deposit or loan euro-dollars seek extra protection against the deterioration of the dollar against other currencies. Figure 8.8 shows the monthly average for the 3-month LIBOR rate and the monthly average yield for 3-month Treasury bills on the secondary market from 2000 to 2010. The graphs indicate a modest TED spread for most of that decade, until the subprime mortgage crisis threatened the entire financial system in 2008. After actions taken by the Federal Reserve and incoming Obama administration calmed fears, the LIBOR rate dropped down close to the Treasury bill yield.

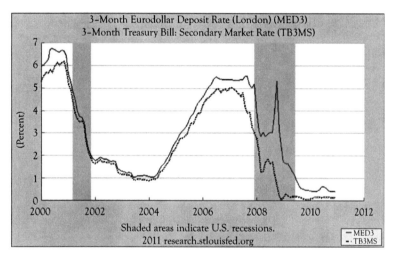

Figure 8.8. Average monthly rates for 3-month eurodollar deposits and 3-month U.S. treasury bills (secondary market) from 2000 to 2010. (Source: Federal Reserve Bank of St. Louis, FRED Economic Data.)

CHAPTER 9

Indicators of Fiscal and Monetary Policy

Government officials and economists who guide macroeconomic policy monitor the same economic indicators as executives and managers in the private and nonprofit sectors. To understand the significance of any economic indicator report, one should not only assess what the reported indicator values say about the state and direction of the economy, but also gauge how those in charge of macroeconomic policy might respond. For example, a report that indicates an unexpected jump in the unemployment rate may lead the Federal Reserve to take action to lower interest rates.

There are two major types of macroeconomic policy: fiscal policy and monetary policy. Changes in these policies may be triggered by economic indicator reports, which in turn result in changes in the economy that will be reflected in future economic indicator values.

Fiscal policy is the collection of actions by government that direct the stream of revenues coming to the government and expenditures made by the government. These activities are usually planned in annual budgets. In the United States, budgets are prepared and monitored by the executive branch under the President, although Congress has approval authority over budgets. Budgets are not necessarily balanced, even in the planning stages, meaning that the expenditures during a year may not be offset by revenues. When expenditures exceed revenues, there is a *budget deficit*. The shortfall in revenues during a budget deficit must be covered by either past savings or borrowing. When revenues exceed expenditures, there is a *budget surplus*. The excess revenues can either be set aside as savings or used to pay down past debt.

When the government runs a deficit, the reaction is largely stimulative in the sense that the government is acting in the role of a net purchaser and putting more money in the hands of individuals and businesses that they can spend. When the government runs a surplus, there is a suppressive effect because the government is taking more away from individuals and businesses and not spending all of it.

For many years, the U.S. federal government has borrowed money as a means of covering deficits. When deficit spending continues over successive years, there is no surplus to repay these loans when they come due, and these loans can only be repaid by taking out additional loans. The accumulation of amounts owed by the government at any given time is the *national debt*. In the case of the United States, this national debt has grown dramatically and is one of the long-term economic challenges that we will discuss in this chapter.

Monetary policy is related to the supply of money in the economy and the ease with which individuals and businesses can borrow. Money is a lubricant in economic transactions, so when money is in ready supply or easy to borrow, there is a stimulating effect. In the United States, monetary policy is largely entrusted to the Federal Reserve System.

The Federal Reserve was created in 1913 to stabilize the financial system of the United States and act as a central bank. The nation had experienced periodic financial panics that, although fairly short in duration, overwhelmed banks as their worried creditors demanded deposits. This mission was expanded in the 1930s following the collapse of the financial system starting in the late 1920s, when the Federal Reserve was assigned to regulate banks against reckless conduct. In the 1970s, the mission was further expanded to conduct monetary policy to achieve "maximum employment, stable prices, and moderate long-term interest rates."[1]

The Federal Reserve has multiple tools that can influence money supply and the cost of borrowing. The Federal Reserve is authorized to set the reserve requirements of banks, which is the percentage of deposits that the bank is required to have on hand overnight rather than out in circulation as loans. Banks often meet their reserve requirements by borrowing from other banks or the Federal Reserve, and the Federal Reserve largely controls the interest rate on those overnight loans. The Federal Reserve is also a major creditor to the U.S. Government as the owner of Treasury bills, notes, and bonds. The Federal Reserve can either buy or sell these debt instruments, and due to its strong presence in these bond markets, is able to drive interest rates higher or lower.

As noted above, the officials charged with managing fiscal and monetary policy and their advisors consult economic indicators of economic activity, income and expenditure, price levels, interest rates, resource utilization, and international exchange. However, there are some additional indicators designed to monitor the conduct of macroeconomic policy. A few of these indicators are discussed in this chapter.

Budget Surplus/Deficit

Most governments budget operations on an annual basis. Although state and local governments have a sizeable impact on local and regional economies, since the 1930s the federal government has been the dominant public economic influence for most Americans and American businesses. The federal government is unique in being able to operate – and intending to operate – at a deficit or surplus, while state and local governments are generally expected to operate with a balanced budget. Consequently, the federal government plays the dominant role in U.S. fiscal policy.

For much of its early history, the federal government ran balanced budgets. The main exceptions occurred in times of war, when the government borrowed money by issuing war bonds and then paying them off in the years following. A major change came in the 1930s, when in response to the Great Depression the administration of Franklin Delano Roosevelt undertook an ambitious program of public projects to deal with the massive underemployment rate of nearly 25%, even higher in the cities. The success of this program was not only in reducing the ranks of the unemployed, but stimulating other sectors of the economy because those hired by the federal projects had more money to spend, thus generating more activity in the private sector, and gradually encouraging more private investment. The economic recovery act in 2009 is a recent instance of attempting to stimulate the economy through increased public expenditure.

The role of deficit spending in stimulating the economy was analyzed in the famous text by John Maynard Keynes, *The General Theory of Employment, Interest, and Money.*[2] In this text, Keynes introduced the concept of a fiscal multiplier as the amount of economic activity generated by a dollar of government expenditure. Keynes advocated that governments should run deficits when the economy contracts to diminish the severity, while running surpluses in times of expansion to offset the deficits in other years, limit inflation, and prevent the economy from setting itself up for a larger contraction. This philosophy dominated macroeconomic policy for the next 40 years, until the limits of this policy were realized in the 1970s when both high unemployment and high inflation occurred at the same time.

Prior to Keynes' text, the prevailing view among economists was that market dynamics would eventually address problems in the economy without strong government intervention. This school of thought, now known as *classical economics*, recognized that short-term imbalances may result from time to time, but in the long-run the supply of productive resources (land, labor, and capital) and the demand for productive resources would come into balance. After the failure of Keynesian-based policy to address the problems of the 1970s, a new school of economic thought emerged that returned to these classical foundations in explaining the limitations of Keynesian fiscal policy in controlling the economy. As we cited in chapter 1, the actions of private parties in anticipation of future government policy measures can distort the desired effect of those measures.

In the 1980s, and again in the 2000s, the United States instituted a variant of fiscal policy based on reducing taxes, rather than increasing expenditures. This idea, called supply-side economics, presumed that reductions in income taxes would stimulate more consumption and more investment. This policy incurs deficits, at least in the short term, because taxes are the main source of revenue to the federal government. The intended result of the policy is that increased consumption and investment will follow, resulting in increased tax revenues and budget surpluses.

The budget for the federal government operates on a fiscal year from October to September. The budget is proposed by the executive branch and prepared by the Office of Management and Budget in February. The budget is supported by the *Economic Report by the President*,[3] which is prepared by the President's Council of Economic Advisors, in which the state of the economy is reviewed and the case is made for the budget. Congress receives, reviews, and approves the budget for the next fiscal year, with assistance from the Congressional Budget Office. The President can sign or veto the budget.

The initial budget and budget negotiations provide a useful indicator of what is likely to follow in the general economy. If the government intends to run a greater deficit, there is an expectation of economic activity, particularly in those sectors targeted with expenditure increases or tax decreases. Similarly, if the deficit is reduced, as it was in the 1990s when defense expenditures were reduced and taxes were increased, these measures signal reduced spending by those affected by tax increases or those sectors that will be receiving less consumption by the government.

It is worth noting the planned budget deficit or surplus is not determined strictly on the basis of Keynesian analysis of the appropriate response to the nation's position in its economic cycle. Although proposals for increased deficits may be justified by the logic of Keynesian stimulus, as was the case in the American Recovery and Investment Act of 2009, deficits often occur because Congress and the President are unwilling to reduce the amounts previously allocated to federal programs. Thus, U.S. fiscal policy is as much (or more) a consequence of legislative compromise as it is a designed program of government income and spending based on economic reasoning.

The Department of the Treasury manages the receipts and outlays to and from the federal government. If a budget deficit is planned, this department will need to borrow money in form of bills, notes, and bonds to make up the difference. If a budget surplus is planned, borrowing activity will be reduced, although some borrowing will continue to take care of maturing debt and handle temporary excesses in expenditures over receipts. The expectation of changes in the borrowing practices of the Treasury Department will indicate upward or downward pressure on interest rates.

Realized Surplus/Deficit

The adopted budget indicates the intended surplus or deficit, but the actual surplus or deficit will vary. Items like unexpected military expenditures and expenses from responding to large natural disasters can exceed the allotments in the original budget. Other items like unexpectedly high tax revenues or lower interest on public debt can create a surplus or reduce the expected deficit.

The Financial Management Service of the Treasury Department issues a *Monthly Treasury Statement* on the eighth business day of each month to report on actual receipts and outlays for the previous month.[4] The summary of the report indicates total receipts and total outlays for the month and fiscal year to date. These are compared to the total amount budgeted for the year and up to that month in the fiscal year. The report also breaks down receipts and outlays by federal department or agency, and even by type of receipt or outlay within agencies.

A number of public agencies, such as the Social Security Administration and the Postal Service, are regarded as "off-budget" even though there are transactions between these agencies and other "on-budget" agencies. These "off-budget" receipts and outlays are detailed in the *Monthly Treasury Statement*, but grouped separately in the summary values.

Figure 9.1 shows the annual federal surplus or deficit from 1970 through 2010. As described in the previous section, deficits have grown over this period, with a temporary reversal in the 1990s from the peace dividend and income tax increases.

The *Monthly Treasury Statement* is of interest to watchdog groups that monitor government activity. However, this report also provides a glimpse as to whether the deficit (or surplus) will be better or worse than expected.

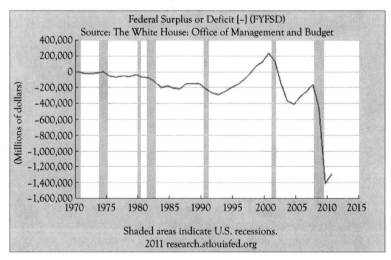

Figure 9.1. Annual federal surplus or deficit from 1970 to 2010. (Source: Federal Reserve Bank of St. Louis, FRED Economic Data.)

Tax Policy

The main source of revenue for the federal government is taxes. The largest source of tax revenue is personal income taxes. The second largest source is taxes on corporate profits, although this amount is substantially less than the revenue from personal income taxes. The third largest source is from federal excise taxes on items like cigarettes. Other revenues come from estate taxes, gift taxes, and customs duties.

Fiscal policy based on Keynesian theory supports the reduction of taxes and the increase of public expenditure to offset economic contractions, because it leaves individuals and businesses with more money to spend, which can stimulate the economy through the multiplier effect. Unfortunately, it is easier for political leaders to embrace this portion of Keynesian theory than the prescription to raise taxes or reduce expenditures when the economy regains upward momentum. As a consequence, the United States has largely run deficits most of the last 50 years, even though the economy was growing most of those years.

Deficits can be reduced by increasing taxes or reducing outlays. However, some outlays cannot be reduced and other reductions would need to be phased in. Still other outlays are targeted to specific sectors of the economy and their reduction would be borne unevenly. In comparison, changes in current tax rates tend to be both more immediate and affect the general economy directly. Modifications to tax laws are a useful indicator of a shift in fiscal policy that will have a prompt impact on economic activity.

Additionally, due to deductibility of some expenses from taxable income, the taxpayer will assess the cost of those tax-deductible items on an after-tax basis:

$$after\text{-}tax\ cost = cost \cdot (1 - marginal\ tax\ rate)$$

If a taxpayer has a marginal federal income tax rate of 28%, a deductible expense of $1000 will be regarded by the taxpayer to be $720, net of tax savings. Interest received or paid by a taxpayer will similarly appear to be at a lower rate if the interest income is taxable or the interest expense is deductible. As a consequence, the tax provisions regarding deductibility of expenses and taxability of income become an element of fiscal policy.

Social Insurance Programs

Social security is the largest off-budget federal program, which is funded by an insurance-like arrangement. Social security tax revenue is actually considerably higher than corporate income tax revenue, although social security tax revenue is to be applied against social security outlays or invested in federal debt as a method of saving for future payments. However, the program design does not assure that promised social security payments will always be covered by social security tax revenues or reserves. Currently, net social security reserves are only growing due to interest earned on those reserves. By the 2030s, the system is projected to have insufficient reserves to make the full promised payments, when the federal government will need to make up the difference or change the payment levels.

Medicare revenue to the federal government is also substantial. Unlike Social Security, Medicare is set up on a pay-as-you-go system where current workers pay the benefits to current seniors. Although a trust fund was built from excess payroll revenues for Medicare in the early years of the program, the program is currently running at a deficit. With the demographic effects of the baby boomer retirements, this system is projected to exhaust its trust funds within 10–20 years.

These programs will have major deficits and debt levels in the decades to come. Under projections by the Congressional Budget Office, outlays for Social Security and federal health care programs like Medicare are currently 10% of the GDP and will grow to 16% of the GDP in the next 25 years.[5] Changes in either the taxation of income to support these programs or promised payoffs will be a key indicator of the future environment for fiscal policy.

Public Debt

The consequence of decades of federal deficits is the accumulation of an enormous public debt. In 2011, the total debt of U.S. government exceeded 14 trillion dollars. About 30% of this debt consists of loans from other federal agencies, most notably the Social Security trust fund, but approximately 70% comes from private creditors, both domestic and foreign.

The borrowing activity in the United States is managed by the Bureau of Public Debt in the U.S. Department of the Treasury. The bureau provides a daily update on the amount of public debt on its website,[6] showing the amount of debt from borrowing outside the government and borrowing from other federal agencies. End-of-period levels of public debt for recent months and years appear in the quarterly *Treasury Bulletin*.[7]

Due to inflation and the growth of the economy in terms of population and productivity, it is not unreasonable for the amount of public debt to have increased. However, when viewed in relation to annual GDP in the same year, the amount of public debt has increased from less than 40% of annual GDP in 1965 to nearly equal to annual GDP in 2011. On average, public debt has grown at an annual rate about 2% higher than the annual rate of growth in GDP. The growth in public debt was particularly high in the 1980s and 2000s, when the United States cut tax rates and increased defense spending. Figure 9.2 shows the growth in total public debt from 1970 to 2010.

The increased debt relative to GDP strains the flexibility of both fiscal policy and monetary policy to keep the economy out of recession. The outlay for net interest on federal government debt has grown to over 6% of the budget, despite interest rates that are at 50-year lows. A further

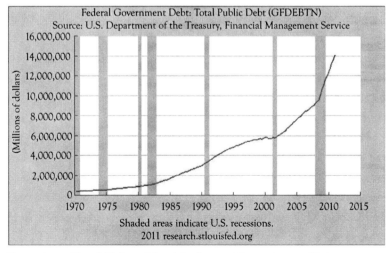

Figure 9.2. Total U.S. public debt from 1970 to 2010. (Source: Federal Reserve Bank of St. Louis, FRED Economic Data.)

increase in debt or an increase in interest rates would make this net interest outlay percent even higher, requiring either more borrowing or austere fiscal discipline in the form of significantly higher taxes and significantly lower government services. The U.S. public is concerned about the burden of public debt on future generations and their elected legislators are resisting authorizing more debt. Holders of U.S. debt, especially foreign creditors, will be increasingly uneasy with the ability of the United States to cover its interest payments and repay principal on maturity, putting further upward pressure on borrowing costs.

FOMC Directives

The main tool used by the Federal Reserve in implementing monetary policy is the purchase and sales of Treasury securities. The Federal Reserve issues instructions to the Federal Reserve Bank of New York to act as its agent in these transactions. These decisions are made by a committee consisting of the Federal Reserve Board of Governors and four presidents from the twelve regional banks in the Federal Reserve System, known as the Federal Open Market Committee (FOMC.) This group schedules eight regular meetings a year, with additional meetings if necessary.

If the Federal Reserve buys Treasury securities, they increase the demand from buyers of the debt, resulting in downward pressure on interest rates. When the transactions are completed, the cash to the seller of the securities is more money in the hands of the public. Further, often the proceeds of these purchases by the Federal Reserve remain as bank deposits of major banks that are able to use those to help meet their reserve requirements and have more money to lend. Thus, purchase operations are stimulative.

When the Federal Reserve sells Treasury debt it owns, the effect is the reverse. Increased seller supply pushes bond prices down and interest rates up. The outside parties that buy the securities from the Federal Reserve need to give up use of their funds, which forces banks that hold the deposits of these buyers to make up their overnight reserves from other sources.

The FOMC reviews the current economic situation and decides on a strategy to either buy or sell a certain amount of debt or do so with a goal in terms of interest rates. The usual interest rate goal is a target, or target range, for the federal funds rate discussed in chapter 6.

The FOMC decision is released in a public statement at the conclusion of the meeting.[8] Minutes of the FOMC are provided to the public about three weeks after the meeting. The minutes can provide more insight into the reasoning behind the decision and what the committee may be watching or inclined to do in the upcoming meetings. The report also includes an addendum that provides projections of changes in real GDP, unemployment rate, PCE inflation, and core PCE inflation in the current year, the next two years, and beyond. These projections are based on forecasts by the members of the Federal Reserve Board and the presidents of the 12 Federal Reserve Banks.

Money Supply

The supply of "money" is considerably more than the amount of currency in circulation in the form of paper bills (Federal Reserve notes) and coins. For example, if someone deposits cash in a checking account, the bank can loan that cash out to someone else, but the original depositor believes he has the funds on account to spend. Consequently, the money supply is really the amount private parties believe they have on hand to spend, rather than the physical currency in their possession.

Money supply is not fully under the control of the Federal Reserve or U.S. Treasury. Money supply is determined by individual saving habits, business activity, and bank behavior. Even hard currency, though printed by the Treasury and distributed by the Federal Reserve, enters the economy when currency is requested by banks according to their operational needs, and is returned to the Federal Reserve and taken out of circulation when banks have more currency than needed. However, these activities by individuals, businesses, and banks are influenced by the Federal Reserve in its open market operations and setting of bank reserve requirements.

There are actually multiple measures of money supply, which are reported weekly by the Federal Reserve.[9] A narrower measure, called *M1*, includes currency in circulation (not in vaults of the Federal Reserve or its depository members) and demand deposits like checking accounts. A broader measure, called *M2*, includes M1, as well as savings deposits, money market balances for individuals, and small time deposits like bank certificates of deposit. The money supply levels are reported with and without seasonal adjustments. Figure 9.3 shows the seasonally adjusted M1 and M2 stocks from 1985 to 2010. Note that M2 levels during this time period were considerably higher than M1 levels and grew at a faster rate.

The Federal Reserve had previously reported another measure of money supply called *M3*, which included M2, along with large time deposits, institutional money market balances, and other liquid assets held by institutions. The Federal Reserve decided M3 was not providing much information for purposes of guiding monetary policy.

There is a theory in economics, called the *quantity theory of money*, which postulates that price levels are linked to the supply of money.[10] This theory was dismissed by Keynesian macroeconomists. However, following the limitations of Keynesian fiscal policy in dealing with joint high unemployment and high inflation in the 1970s, money supply regained attention as a key contributing factor in inflation. Nobel laureate Milton Friedman was a strong proponent of this view even prior to the 1970s and

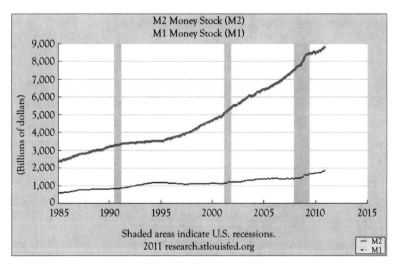

Figure 9.3. M1 and M2 money stocks, seasonally adjusted, from 1985 to 2010. The higher, thicker line is the M2 stock level. (Source: Federal Reserve Bank of St. Louis, FRED Economic Data.)

claimed that inflation would not be a problem if the growth in money supply were linked to the growth in the GDP.[11]

Currently the Federal Reserve sets targets in terms of the federal funds rate rather than money supply. However, money supply is still a useful indicator of the effectiveness of monetary policy and future actions by the FOMC.

The Beige Book

Prior to each of the eight scheduled FOMC meetings, the Federal Reserve Bank in Boston prepares a report, known as the Beige Book, that summarizes economic conditions in each of the twelve Federal Reserve Districts.[12] The report assesses the strength of consumer demand, employment conditions, developments in the major business sectors, and the status of credit and borrowing in that district. The content is largely anecdotal observations gathered from conversations with business leaders and economists, rather than the product of rigorous data collection and statistical analysis.

The Beige Book is reviewed carefully by the FOMC committee prior to its meeting. The report is available to the public about two weeks prior to the FOMC meeting, giving investors an advance look at the environment as seen by the FOMC and likely action by the committee. In addition, the report is of interest to others who would like a verbal briefing on recent changes in economic conditions in different regions of the nation.

Bank Lending Practices

Banks and other lending organizations play a key role in the effectiveness of monetary policy. These institutions are the intermediaries between the Federal Reserve and the rest of the economy. The success of the goals of the Federal Reserve in influencing interest rates and stimulating economic activity depends on the banks and other lenders adjusting the interest rates they charge accordingly and their willingness to extend credit to households and businesses.

To gauge the current trends with banks, the Federal Reserve conducts a quarterly survey of senior loan officers of domestic banks and U.S. branches of foreign banks.[13] The results of the survey inform the FOMC committee in its deliberations.

The sample lending officers are asked a number of questions related to terms and qualification criteria for loans and strength of customer demand. The questions are asked for different types of loans, including loans to large businesses, small businesses, and households, as well as for commercial real estate, home mortgages, auto loans, and credit cards. Questions are similar to those used in preparing a diffusion index, where the respondent is asked whether some aspect of a particular type of loan strengthened or tightened considerably, strengthened or tightened moderately, is about the same, weakened or eased moderately, or weakened or eased considerably. The collective responses to any item are summarized by subtracting the percentage who reported the item weakened or eased from the percentage who reported the item strengthened or tightened.

Figure 9.4 shows the net percentage reporting that standards for commercial and industrial loans for large and medium size firms tightened over the past three months, for quarters in 1990 through 2010. Note that the standards usually tighten during recessions, when there is greater risk of default by borrowers due to the weak economy.

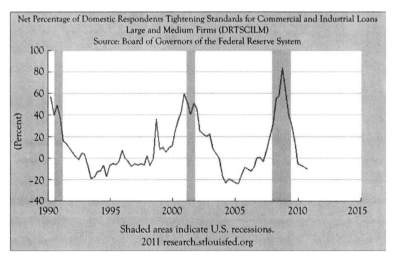

Figure 9.4. Net percentage of domestic respondents to Federal Reserve senior loan officer survey who reported tightened loan standards for large and medium industrial and commercial firms, quarterly and not seasonally adjusted, from 1990 to 2010. (Source: Federal Reserve Bank of St. Louis, FRED Economic Data.)

CHAPTER 10

Sources of Economic Indicator Data

Prior to the Internet, access to economic indicator data was limited to brief reports in the business media or printed reports by the U.S. government. Government reports were published at the Government Printing Office and then physically distributed, which resulted in delays for many users. The reports were available by subscription at some cost or required use of one of the designated Federal Repository Libraries that store government documents. There was limited access to data in electronic form from some data services that prepared and distributed databases, but these were often incomplete and somewhat dated when received.

The U.S. government has embraced the Internet as a means of providing economic indicators and commentary to the public, as have other organizations that prepare widely tracked indicators. The challenge has changed from the data being difficult to obtain and incomplete, to one of finding the best sources and filtering the high volume of readily available and usually free data online. This chapter cites some good sources that assist in accessing the key data and interpreting those data. The chapter concludes with some guidelines for designing your own program of monitoring economic indicators.

Websites with Economic Calendars

A useful tool for monitoring and learning about U.S. economic indicators is to find a website that reports recent announcements of major indicators. Fortunately, some financial websites provide this service, organizing the indicators by the date on which they were announced or will be announced, in the format of an *economic calendar*.

These financial websites are affiliated with Web portals like Yahoo! and MSN or websites for financial media like Bloomberg and *The Wall Street Journal*. These sites provide one-stop locations for data related to financial markets and include economic calendars as part of that service. However, for economic indicator data, these sites are often a vehicle for other services like Econoday.com and Briefing.com, which access, store, and present the data. In this section we will cite some of these websites and their providers, with some commentary on the relative strengths and weaknesses of each. Direct link addresses for these sites appear in the references, with citations to the references in the endnotes, but the reader is asked to bear in mind that these links and the content of these websites are subject to change.

Bloomberg, a major provider of data to the financial industry, provides a well-designed economic calendar.[1] The main economic calendar page is easy to find from the main Bloomberg.com page under the "Markets" menu. The design and content of the economic indicators portion of the website is provided by Econoday. The calendar is presented in the form of a conventional calendar with a row devoted to each week and block within the row for each business day in that week. The user can look at the current week or all weeks in a month.

Within the calendar block for any day, the key U.S. indicators announced that day are listed. Most of the listed indicators have hyperlinks to pages devoted to the current announcement for that indicator. Prior to the announcement, the page for an indicator shows the previous value of the indicator, plus the consensus forecast and consensus range for where the newly announced value of that indicator is likely to be. After the indicator has been announced, the announced value is filled in, as well as any revision to the previous value. Some commentary on the recent announcement is added. The individual announcement pages have links labeled "Why Investors Care," which assess the significance of this indicator.

The Econoday-powered Bloomberg economic calendar includes a page of release dates for economic indicator announcements for the current year, organized alphabetically by indicator. When clicking an indicator in the list, the user is taken to the page that described the result of that announcement. The economic calendar site also includes a listing of the indicators organized in groups entitled Market Moving Indicators, Merit Extra Attention Indicators, Other Key Indicators, and Treasury Events. Many of these indicators, especially those in the first two groups, are described in this text.

The Wall Street Journal's website, online.wsj.com, offers an economic calendar[2] that is very similar to the Bloomberg.com calendar because the source of the economic indicator content is also Econoday. Navigating to the economic calendar webpage is slightly more involved than on the Bloomberg site: the user needs to access the Market Data Center from the Markets menu, then find the Calendars & Economy summary on the page, and finally click the link to "See Full Economic Calendar." Once this page is accessed, the organization and content is similar to that on the Bloomberg site.

The wsj.com economic indicators site has two features that the Bloomberg site does not provide. One is a calendar of key indicator announcements from other nations. Another feature is an Economic Indicators Archive page.[3] This page lists about 30 of the key indicators, followed by a brief description of each and a link to a pdf file of the formal announcement by the agency or organization that prepares the economic indicator.

The Web portal Yahoo! offers an economic calendar on the finance portion of its website.[4] Users can navigate to the economic calendar page from the main finance page by selecting "Market Overview" from the main Investing menu and then selecting "Economic Calendar" from the list of "Market Events" at the bottom of the page. The economic indicator data on this site is provided by the service Briefing.com. The indicators are presented in the form of a list of indicators for the current week, but the user can click links to look at the list for a previous week or the upcoming week.

Each indicator on the Yahoo! Finance calendar is described on a single line showing the date of the announcement, the previous value, the pre-announcement market consensus, and the preannouncement Briefing.com forecast. After the formal announcement, the announced value and any revision of the previous value are added. A few key indicators have hyperlinks to pages with a brief description of the indicator, the agency or organization providing it, a grade of its importance, when in a monthly or quarterly cycle the announcement is released, and a link to access raw data.

MSN's moneycentral.msn.com site provides an economic data calendar[5] powered by Briefing.com. However, on this website the indicators are listed by month, rather than by week, and the list is rather long. Also, the MSN site does not have hyperlinks for further detail on any of the indicators. Another drawback of the MSN economic calendar is that it is difficult to access using hyperlinks. The user is better off doing a search for "economic calendar" within msn.com to find the link.

The content from Econoday.com and Briefing.com can be accessed directly. The content is not significantly different than what can be accessed on the portals, although the organization on the Briefing.com site is improved over the organizations found on Yahoo! Finance or MSN Moneycentral by including all the indicators to be announced in a month organized by week.

Sources of Downloadable Data

Economic indicator announcements generally focus on recent indicator values. To determine the indicator values for earlier periods or to access the entire time series for an indicator, a user needs to access either the website for the preparing agency of the economic indicator, obtain print reports from the printing office of the preparing agency, or use a source that collects and reports economic indicator time series data.

Many sites provide time series data in forms that can be downloaded into software that can display and process the data, such as in the form of an Excel file or a csv (comma-separated values) file. Government agencies provide these data files for download at no charge, but some private organizations do charge for the data or require a membership for access. The best way to look for a specific time series is to go the website for the agency that prepares the indicator, find the page dedicated to the announcements for that indicator and look for a link for data in a downloadable format.

Some websites collect and provide data from several preparing agencies and provide the data either in the form of a graph or a table. Users can also download data for their own use on their software. We include brief descriptions of two of the more impressive websites that offer this service.

The Federal Reserve Bank of St. Louis maintains an online Federal Reserve Economic Data (FRED) service with a broad collection of time series data for economic indicators.[6] Nearly all of the figures in this text are graphs we gratefully obtained, and often customized online, by working with this website. The data are organized in 16 major categories. Each major category is broken into subcategories with lists of related indicators from federal agencies and several outside sources. The lists in each subcategory are sorted by popularity, so the indicators most users seek appear often at the top of the list. When an indicator is selected, the user sees a graph of the indicator for the entire time series. Some time series are offered in multiple formats, such as seasonally adjusted and not adjusted, or by week, month, or year. The page for each time series identifies the source, the units of the measure, and a link to the source.

The user can edit the graph considerably. One can transform the data by aggregating time periods (for example, monthly data to annual data) or expressing the time series as an index, as a period-to-period or year-to-year change, as a percentage period-to-period or year-to-year change, or as compound growth rate. The user can restrict the graph to a limited segment of the time series. The color, thickness, and line style can be changed, as can background colors and text fonts. The scale can be changed to a log scale, and the graph can be changed to a bar, scatter, or pie chart.

Multiple time series from the FRED database can be placed on the same graph, with a secondary scale on the right side. The user can also create a customized data transformation, using values from multiple time series in the transformation formulas.

Another nice feature of the FRED graphs is that gray bands automatically appear to show periods of recession as designated by the NBER. These "recession bars" can be turned off, but are helpful in interpreting patterns on the graphs.

Users can download the data to an Excel spreadsheet, print it locally on a printer or to an Adobe Acrobat pdf file, or copy a link to the page. Users can also register with the site to be able to save graphs and settings for graphs.

The Bureau of Economic Analysis (BEA) has been cited frequently in this text as the provider of several key economic indicators. The BEA is responsible for estimating GDP and components of the GDP. The BEA estimates income to and outlays by households and business sectors. This agency also tracks the international balance of payments and international investments that cross the U.S. border. As such, the BEA is one of the most important sources of economic data.

In addition to providing links to download selected tables as Excel files, the BEA provides access to a large number of its tables via a facility on its website called "Interactive Data."[7] First, a user selects a table from a vast online catalog to explore. Using the "Options" in the facility, the user designates which years to display in the table and whether to display quarterly data or annual data. The table can be downloaded to the user's computer in one of multiple common file formats or printed on the user's local printer.

Individual line items, or multiple line items in the selected table can be displayed on a chart within the Interactive Data system. The chart can be a line or a bar chart. When placing the cursor over points on the chart, the time period at that location on the graph is identified with a sliding vertical line and the value of the indicator on the line or bar pops up when the cursor is located there. A control below the chart allows the user to readily adjust the first and last time period displayed on the chart. The chart can be blown up to full screen, printed on the user's printer, or downloaded as a png graphics file.

As with the FRED system, users can register and open an account on the BEA Interactive Data website. Registering an account allows a user to save work for later access.

Printed Reports Discussing Economic Indicators

Online economic calendars provide a means of viewing recent reports of key economic indicators in one place. These sites are particularly helpful to investors, who need to respond to these announcements before the rest of the market has reacted. However, these sites often present data for only a few periods, or a year at most. The reports on the economic calendar websites tend to present just one or two key numbers from the original agency report and provide limited commentary on the trend and significance of the measure.

Fortunately, the federal government prepares reports that provide several values of an indicator time series in tables and graphs. While these reports are not as immediate as the indicator announcements on economic calendar sites, they provide a good resource for understanding the state of the economy. In this section, we will identify five of these reports that merit special attention. While all of these documents are formally printed, they are also available as free downloads from the URLs identified in the reference section of this text.

The Council of Economic Advisors, which is part of the executive branch of the government and advises the President, prepares a monthly report, entitled *Economic Indicators*.[8] The named recipient of the report is the Joint Economic Committee of Congress. The report shows about 10 years of data for several economic indicators in tabular form, with key indicators also shown as graphs. The tables address the major areas of the economy: output, income, and spending; employment, unemployment, and wages; production and business activity; prices; money, credit, and security markets; personal finance; international statistics. Although the report contains very little discussion of the data, it is an excellent source for reviewing the spectrum of key economic indicators within a fairly compact document.

The Bureau of Economic Analysis (BEA) produces a monthly publication, entitled *Survey of Current Business*.[9] While not all data collection activity of the BEA is addressed in every issue, the articles in each issue report on some of the ongoing data collection programs, with tables and commentary. The online version provides links to Excel files of tables and to BEA's Interactive Data facility described above. The articles provide some insight into how the BEA collects data and deals with the challenges of developing valid and reliable estimates.

The Bureau of Labor Statistics (BLS) in the Department of Labor is the key source for data related to employment, wages, productivity, and consumer and producer prices (including imports and export prices.) The bureau produces a monthly publication, entitled *Monthly Labor Review*,[10] which includes a few analytical articles related to labor issues, but concludes with several pages of tables related to its data collection and reporting activities. There is no accompanying commentary with the tables, but the tables are comprehensive of BLS data-gathering programs. Approximately ten years of quarterly or annual data are presented for some measures, but only two or three years of data are listed for other measures.

The Council of Economic Advisors prepares an assessment of the nation's economic condition and future challenges in the annual *Economic Report of the President*.[11] This report follows soon after the President's proposal of the nation's next budget. This report contains a considerable amount of commentary, supported by charts of key economic indicators. The commentary favors the view of the current administration, but none-theless provides the reader with an excellent orientation to the state of the economy. The appendix of the report includes a comprehensive set of statistical tables that cover the major economic indicators, broken down into key components.

As noted in chapter 8, monetary policy in the United States is largely entrusted to the Federal Reserve System. Twice a year, the Board of Gover-nors prepares a *Monetary Report to Congress*[12] to accompany testimony by the Chairman of the Federal Reserve Board of Governor to Congress. The printed report provides a chapter on the state of the economy, especially the state of financial institutions. Another chapter assesses the conduct of monetary policy in recent months and anticipates monetary policy issues in future months. The final chapter provides projections of future condi-tions that are prepared for the Federal Open Market Committee. This report is fairly brief and provides a very good overview of the economy from the perspective of monetary policy.

Economic Indicators for U.S. Regions, U.S. States, and Other Nations

The focus of this text has been on economic indicators that characterize the overall U.S. economy. For some readers, the area of interest may be a particular area of the United States, a specific state, or a different nation.

Many federal data collection programs are extensive enough to pro-vide estimates that apply to sections of the United States (for example, the northeast), individual states, and even individual metropolitan areas. For nearly all the key economic indicators discussed in this book, one can find measures that apply to regions, states, and metropolitan areas by consulting the detailed tables that accompany the full reports.

State governments have their own programs for collection and reporting of data, even though the breadth of measures is not as extensive as what is provided by federal agencies. Often these state agencies obtain some of their statistics from the federal government, rather than actually gather and process the data themselves, which not only avoids the expense of duplicated effort, but saves readers the effort of isolating appropriate state-level statistics from the federal sources.

Other nations have programs of data collection and analysis similar to the United States, particularly countries with developed economies. Most of these countries provide reports of recent data values, as well as Internet access to economic indicator time series data. However, that access may be complicated by differences in language or understanding of the organization of data services provided by those governments.

Probably a better means of finding key economic indicators for other nations is from organizations that routinely collect and report this data from several countries. The World Bank has collected a massive amount of international economic data and has facilitated online access by the worldwide public with its Open Data Initiative.[13] The Organisation for Economic Co-operation and Development has a considerable online database of economic and other data for several countries. The International Monetary Fund offers several online databases,[14] including a World Outlook Database that provides values for several of the key indicators discussed in this text, both in terms of reported values in recent years and estimates for upcoming years.

Several international organizations, including those mentioned in the previous paragraph, participate in a joint effort called the Inter-Agency Group on Economic and Financial Statistics. This effort has resulted in an online Principal Global Indicators Database[15] that provides comparable data for several key economic indicators for the nations in the G-20, along with a few other countries. The tables include monthly or quarterly values for past one or two years and annual data for the past five to ten years.

Customizing Your Own Economic Indicator Tracking System

Checking the status of recent indicator announcements on an economic calendar website or reading reports of the general state of the nation's economy in terms of these indicators are useful practices for keeping track of the developments in the overall economy. Since the performance of almost any business is correlated to some degree with measures of economic activity, price levels, interest rates, and resource utilization for the national economy, keeping abreast of general economic indicators will alert a manager to potential opportunities or problems.

However, some economic indicators are more pertinent to a particular business or organization than others. Just as one benefits by eating the right foods in the right amounts, it is probably better to limit your intake of the virtually limitless supply of indicator data and focus on the measures that are effective in anticipating changes to your own business environment and guiding you to better decisions. This final section offers some suggestions for designing your own list of indicators that you should track regularly.

When you read an indicator announcement, think carefully about how a change in that indicator is likely to affect your business. If you can make a good argument for why trends and cycles in that indicator will translate to trends and cycles for your industry and organization, you have probably found a useful indicator to track. If you or someone in your organization has some skills in working with time series data, you can use statistical methods to test the strength of the association between economic indicator values and your organization's performance metrics.[16]

In considering candidate indicators to track regularly, give special attention to leading indicators. As described in chapter 3, leading indicators usually change direction in advance of changes in the direction of the business cycle. A good group of indicators to consider is the 10 indicators used in the Leading Economic Index prepared by The Conference Board: Examine each of those indicators to see which ones seem most relevant to your operation. Again, time series analysis can confirm the statistical strength of any association, but if there seems to be an obvious connection, a leading indicator for the GDP will probably be a leading indicator for your metrics. Another good source of leading indicators are measures that apply to sectors that are upstream or downstream from your organization's position in its value chain, as recent changes in production, demand, and prices in those sectors are likely to impact your organization shortly.

Chances are good that you are not the first person in your industry or function within your industry to look for available indicators that signal changes in your business environment. Take a look at trade publications that target your industry or markets and see which indicators they cite or reproduce in their reports. Along with discovering relevant indicators and sources of time series data, you may find a convenient medium for tracking conditions for your industry.

While the coverage of economic indicators in this text focused on national measures, we mentioned that many of these reports disaggregate the data and report the indicator values for specific geographic areas, business sectors, or demographic groups. Linking to the full report accompanying any economic indicator announcement will often provide the statistics that apply to specific regions, subpopulations, or business sectors.

The large volume and dispersed locations of online time series data can make regular access to a specific set of indicators cumbersome. For some online sources, data tables may be directly accessible by finding a web URL that links directly to the table of interest and that URL can be stored as a "favorite" in your browser. However, finding some economic indicator data requires the user to interact with a webpage before the data is provided. Fortunately, some online services are emerging to aid users of these databases. Earlier in this chapter we cited the FRED database provided by the Federal Reserve Bank of St. Louis and the Interactive Data capability on the BEA website. By registering for a free account, users of the FRED system can create and save their own lists of time series that they consult regularly, rather than navigating or searching for each one individually each time they want to view them. The BEA Interactive Data system allows users to save the steps for navigating to a table and user settings for presenting the table in a chart.

Good luck with your economic indicators tracking system!

Notes

Chapter 1

1. A transcript of the Ford–Carter debate can be found online at the Commission on Presidential Debates (1976).
2. The definition of information as a difference appears in Bateson (1972).
3. Formalizations of the notion that public awareness of the use of economic and social indicators by policy-makers will result in actions by outside parties that reduce the effectiveness of these indicators for the purposes of making policy include Goodhart's law, Campbell's law, and the Lucas critique. See Goodhart (1975), Campbell (1976), and Lucas (1976).

Chapter 2

1. Basic techniques for analyzing time series data are presented in Stengel & Chaffe-Stengel (forthcoming).
2. Estimation of seasonal factors and their use in deseasonalizing data and forecasting are covered in Stengel & Chaffe-Stengel (forthcoming).
3. One example of a chained index is the Fisher index, which is the geometric mean of a Laspeyres index and Paasche index. The value is calculated by taking the square root of the product of the Laspeyres index and Paasche index values for each time period.

Chapter 3

1. The recent news release for the GDP and links to the full report and tables appear online at Bureau of Economic Analysis (2011a).
2. Answers to frequently asked questions about the definition of recessions by the NBER appear at National Bureau of Economic Research (2011).
3. The recent press release of the U.S. Leading Economic Index is available at The Conference Board (2011a).
4. The advance, preliminary, and revised retail sales reports are available at U.S. Census Bureau (2011a).
5. The retail sectors included in the GAFO sales are listed at U.S. Census Bureau (2011b).
6. The e-commerce report is available at U.S. Census Bureau (2011c).

7. A report on light vehicle sales can be found online at Autodata Corporation (2011).

8. See the latest Industrial Production Index announcement provided by Board of Governors of the Federal Reserve System (2011a).

9. The latest reports for *Manufacturers' Shipments, Inventories, and Orders* are available at U.S. Census Bureau (2011d).

10. Access the latest ISM reports at Institute for Supply Management (2011).

11. Recent releases of the Business Outlook Survey can be found at Federal Reserve Bank of Philadelphia (2011).

12. The latest report on the Consumer Confidence Index is available at The Conference Board (2011b).

13. Recent Consumer Sentiment Index reports appear at Thomson Reuters (2011).

14. See U.S. Census Bureau (2011e) for reports and data on housing starts.

15. Recent reports on construction spending are available at U.S. Census Bureau (2011f).

Chapter 4

1. Reports on Gross Domestic Income and its components are part of the report on U.S. Gross Domestic Product at Bureau of Economic Analysis (2011a).

2. The recent release and associated tables for personal income are available at Bureau of Economic Analysis (2011b).

3. See Surowiecki (2005).

4. Recent *Income, Poverty and Health Insurance Coverage in the United States* reports can be accessed from a list of links at U.S. Census Bureau (2001g).

5. For a description of the Gini index, see The World Bank (2011a).

6. The report on distribution of net worth in the U.S. for 2007 and earlier years appears in Board of Governors of the Federal Reserve System (2009).

7. For the current table showing the net worth of households and nonprofit organizations, see Board of Governors of the Federal Reserve System (2011b).

Chapter 5

1. The gateway to CPI reports and data on the Internet is at Bureau of Labor Statistics (2011a).

2. For a discussion about the Chained CPI-U, see Bureau of Labor Statistics (2011b).

3. For an overview of the hedonic quality adjustment, see Bureau of Labor Statistics (2011c).

4. The gateway to PPI reports and data on the Internet is at Bureau of Labor Statistics (2011d).

5. The recent Employment Situation report is available at Bureau of Labor Statistics (2011e).

6. The recent Employment Cost Index report appears at Bureau of Labor Statistics (2011f).

7. For the recent report on the S&P/Case-Shiller index, see Standard & Poors (2011).

8. For an explanation of the methodology of the S&P/Case-Shiller index, see the link to "Methodology" at Standard & Poors (2011).

9. See National Association of Realtors (2011) for links to the latest reports on existing home sales and pending home sales.

10. For reports and other links related to new residential sales, see U.S. Census Bureau (2011h).

11. Links to price data for crude oil, gasoline, and other petroleum products are at Energy Information Administration (2011a).

12. Agriculture price data are available at National Agriculture Statistics Service (2011).

Chapter 6

1. See Board of Governors of the Federal Reserve System (2011c) for more detail about reserve requirements.

2. A description of the operation of auctions for treasury securities is at TreasuryDirect (2011a).

3. A table of municipal bond yields for different maturities appears in Bloomberg (2011a).

4. For more details about the COFI, see Federal Home Loan Bank of San Francisco (2011).

5. The recent report on consumer credit interest rates is available at Board of Governors of the Federal Reserve System (2011d).

6. See Bankrate (2011) for typical current home equity loan rates.

Chapter 7

1. The employment summary report is accessible from Bureau of Labor Statistics (2011e).

2. The recent report on unemployment insurance claims and links to data are available at U.S. Department of Labor (2011).

3. Monster Worldwide (2011) provides a description of the index and links to recent monthly reports.

4. See Bureau of Labor Statistics (2011e) for access to the recent average work-week report.

5. Links to releases of productivity reports and data appear at Bureau of Labor Statistics (2011g).

6. Access to news releases and data for multifactor productivity is available at Bureau of Labor Statistics (2011h).

7. This news release can be found at Bureau of Labor Statistics (2011i).

8. The recent report on capacity utilization is at Board of Governors of the Federal Reserve System (2011a).

9. See U.S. Census Bureau (2011i) for access to the latest reports on business inventories.

10. The latest petroleum status report is available at Energy Information Administration (2011b).

11. The latest natural gas storage report is available at Energy Information Administration (2011c).

Chapter 8

1. Bureau of Economic Analysis (2011c) provides the latest news release for imports and exports, with links to tables and data files.

2. See Bureau of Labor Statistics (2011j) for access to releases and data pertaining to the import and export price indexes.

3. Trade weighted foreign exchange index releases and data are available at Board of Governors of the Federal Reserve System (2011e).

4. Bureau of Economic Analysis (2011d) provides the latest news release for international transactions, with links to tables and data files.

5. For a detailed explanation about U.S. international transaction accounts, see Bach (2010).

6. Press releases and data from the Treasury international capital system are available from U.S. Department of the Treasury (2011a).

7. See Bureau of Economic Analysis (2011e) for the recent press release and links to tables.

8. Information about the LIBOR and access to current daily rates is at British Bankers' Association (2011).

Chapter 9

1. A full statement of the mission of the Federal Reserve is at Board of Governors of the Federal Reserve (2011f).

2. This classic text is Keynes (1936).
3. For the recent report, see Council of Economic Advisors (2011a).
4. The current statement is available at Financial Management Service (2011).
5. See Congressional Budget Office (2011) for the report with this discussion.
6. The current level of U.S. public debt is posted at TreasuryDirect (2011b).
7. Access to the current issue and past issues of the *Treasury Bulletin* is available at U.S. Department of the Treasury (2011b).
8. FOMC statements and meeting minutes are provided at Board of Governors of the Federal Reserve System (2011g).
9. For data on money supply measures, see Board of Governors of the Federal Reserve System (2011h).
10. A short description and history of the quantity theory of money appears at Investopedia (2011).
11. See Friedman and Schwartz (1963).
12. Past issues of the Beige Book are available at Board of Governors of the Federal Reserve System (2011i).
13. Results of past surveys are available at Board of Governors of the Federal Reserve System (2011j).

Chapter 10

1. The Bloomberg online economic calendar is available from Bloomberg (2011b).
2. *The Wall Street Journal* online calendar is available from The Wall Street Journal (2011a).
3. See The Wall Street Journal (2011b) for the economic indicators archive.
4. See Yahoo! (2011) for the Yahoo! Finance economic calendar page.
5. The MSN Money economic data calendar is available at Microsoft (2011).
6. The FRED database can be accessed at Federal Reserve Bank of St. Louis (2011).
7. See Bureau of Economic Analysis (2011f) for guidance on the use of its Interactive Data capability.
8. Issues of *Economic Indicators* can be accessed at Council of Economic Advisors (2011b).
9. The recent issue of the *Survey of Current Business* and links to tables are available at Bureau of Economic Analysis (2011g).
10. See Bureau of Labor Statistics (2011k) for the recent issue of *Monthly Labor Review* and access to the archive of past issues.
11. The latest annual economic report of the President is available at Council of Economic Advisors (2011a).

12. Recent semiannual reports on monetary policy can be found at Board of Governors of the Federal Reserve System (2011k).
13. See The World Bank (2011b) for access to its Open Data.
14. Global economic indicators can be accessed at International Monetary Fund (2011).
15. The Principal Global Indicators are available at Inter-Agency Group on Economic & Financial Statistics (2011).
16. Methods of analyzing relationships between time series are addressed in most texts on time series analysis, including Stengel & Chaffe-Stengel (forthcoming).

References

Autodata Corporation (2011). *Motorintelligence.* Retrieved August 9, 2011, from: http://www.motorintelligence.com/m_frameset.html

Bach, C. L. (2010). A guide to the U.S. international transactions accounts and the U.S. international investment position accounts. *Survey of Current Business 90*(2), 33–51.

Bankrate (2011). *Home equity loan rates, news, and advice from bankrate.com.* Retrieved August 11, 2011, from: http://www.bankrate.com/home-equity.aspx

Bateson, G. (1972). Form, substance and difference. In *Steps to an ecology of mind* (pp. 448–464). New York, NY: Ballantine.

Bloomberg (2011a). *U.S. government bonds, treasury & municipal bond yields.* Retrieved August 11, 2011, from: http://www.bloomberg.com/markets/rates-bonds/government-bonds/us/

Bloomberg (2011b). *Economic calendar—Bloomberg.* Retrieved August 13, 2011, from: http://www.bloomberg.com/markets/economic-calendar/

Board of Governors of the Federal Reserve System (2009). Changes in U.S. family finances from 2004 to 2007: Evidence from the survey of consumer finances. *Federal Reserve Bulletin 95*, A1–A56.

Board of Governors of the Federal Reserve System (2011a). *Industrial production and capacity utilization—G.17.* Retrieved August 10, 2011, from: http://www.federalreserve.gov/releases/g17/current/

Board of Governors of the Federal Reserve System (2011b). *Balance sheet of households and nonprofit organizations.* Retrieved August 10, 2011, from: http://www.federalreserve.gov/releases/z1/current/z1r-5.pdf

Board of Governors of the Federal Reserve System (2011c). *FRB—Reserve requirements.* Retrieved August 11, 2011, from: http://www.federalreserve.gov/monetarypolicy/reservereq.htm

Board of Governors of the Federal Reserve System (2011d). *FRB—G.19 Release-Consumer credit.* Retrieved August 11, 2011, from: http://www.federalreserve.gov/releases/g19/current/

Board of Governors of the Federal Reserve System (2011e). *FRB—H.10 Release - Nominal/real indexes.* Retrieved August 12, 2011, from: http://www.federalreserve.gov/releases/h10/summary/default.htm

Board of Governors of the Federal Reserve System (2011f). *FRB—Mission.* Retrieved August 13, 2011, from: http://www.federalreserve.gov/aboutthefed/mission.htm

Board of Governors of the Federal Reserve System (2011g). *FRB—Meeting calendars, statements, and minutes.* Retrieved August 13, 2011, from: http://www.federalreserve.gov/monetarypolicy/fomccalendars.htm

Board of Governors of the Federal Reserve System (2011h). *FRB—H.6 release - Money stock and debt measures.* Retrieved August 13, 2011, from: http://www.federalreserve.gov/releases/h6/current/

Board of Governors of the Federal Reserve System (2011i). *FRB—Beige book.* Retrieved August 13, 2011, from: http://www.federalreserve.gov/FOMC/BeigeBook/

Board of Governors of the Federal Reserve System (2011j). *FRB—Senior loan officer opinion survey on bank lending practices.* Retrieved August 13, 2011, from: http://www.federalreserve.gov/boarddocs/snloansurvey/

Board of Governors of the Federal Reserve System (2011k). *FRB—Monetary policy report to Congress.* Retrieved August 13, 2011, from: http://www.federalreserve.gov/monetarypolicy/mpr_default.htm

British Bankers' Association (2011). *BBA—Libor.* Retrieved August 12, 2011, from: http://www.bbalibor.com/

Bureau of Economic Analysis (2011a). *News release: Gross domestic product.* Retrieved August 9, 2011, from: http://www.bea.gov/newsreleases/national/gdp/gdpnewsrelease.htm

Bureau of Economic Analysis (2011b). *News release: Personal income and outlays.* Retrieved August 10, 2011, from: http://www.bea.gov/newsreleases/national/pi/pinewsrelease.htm

Bureau of Economic Analysis (2011c). *News release: U.S. international trade in goods and services.* Retrieved August 12, 2011, from: http://www.bea.gov/newsreleases/international/trade/tradnewsrelease.htm

Bureau of Economic Analysis (2011d). *News release: U.S. international transactions.* Retrieved August 12, 2011, from: http://www.bea.gov/newsreleases/international/transactions/transnewsrelease.htm

Bureau of Economic Analysis (2011e). *News release: U.S. net international investment position at yearend.* Retrieved August 12, 2011, from: http://www.bea.gov/newsreleases/international/intinv/intinvnewsrelease.htm

Bureau of Economic Analysis (2011f). *Interactive data.* Retrieved August 13, 2011, from: http://www.bea.gov/itable/index.cfm

Bureau of Economic Analysis (2011g). *Survey of current business.* Retrieved August 13, 2011, from: http://www.bea.gov/scb/

Bureau of Labor Statistics (2011a). *Consumer price index (CPI).* Retrieved August 11, 2011, from: http://www.bls.gov/cpi/

Bureau of Labor Statistics (2011b). *Frequently asked questions about the chained consumer price index for all urban consumers (C-CPI-U).* Retrieved August 11, 2011, from: http://www.bls.gov/cpi/cpisupqa.htm

Bureau of Labor Statistics (2011c). *Hedonic quality adjustment in the CPI.* Retrieved August 11, 2011, from: http://www.bls.gov/cpi/cpihqaitem.htm

Bureau of Labor Statistics (2011d). *Producer price index (PPI)*. Retrieved August 11, 2011, from: http://www.bls.gov/ppi/

Bureau of Labor Statistics (2011e). *Employment situation summary*. Retrieved August 11, 2011, from: http://www.bls.gov/news.release/empsit.nr0.htm

Bureau of Labor Statistics (2011f). *Employment cost index news release text*. Retrieved August 11, 2011, from: http://www.bls.gov/news.release/eci.nr0.htm

Bureau of Labor Statistics (2011g). *Labor productivity and costs homepage*. Retrieved August 12, 2011, from: http://www.bls.gov/lpc/

Bureau of Labor Statistics (2011h). *Archived BLS news releases*. Retrieved August 12, 2011, from: http://www.bls.gov/schedule/archives/all_nr.htm#PROD3

Bureau of Labor Statistics (2011i). *Multifactor productivity trends*. Retrieved August 12, 2011, from: http://www.bls.gov/news.release/prod3.toc.htm

Bureau of Labor Statistics (2011j). *Import/export price indexes*. Retrieved August 12, 2011, from: http://www.bls.gov/mxp/

Bureau of Labor Statistics (2011k). *Monthly labor review online*. Retrieved August 13, 2011, from: http://www.bls.gov/mlr/

Campbell, D. (1976). *Assessing the impact of planned social change*. Hanover, NH: Dartmouth College, The Public Affairs Center.

Commission on Presidential Debates (1976). *September 23, 1976 debate transcript*. Retrieved August 9, 2011, from: http://www.debates.org/index.php?page=september-23-1976-debate-transcript

The Conference Board (2011a). *U.S. LEI increases|The Conference Board*. Retrieved August 9, 2011 from: http://www.conference-board.org/data/bcicountry.cfm?cid=1

The Conference Board (2011b). *Consumer confidence index|The Conference Board*. Retrieved August 9, 2011, from: http://www.conference-board.org/data/consumerconfidence.cfm

Congressional Budget Office (2011). *CBO's 2011 long-term budget outlook*. Retrieved August 13, 2011, from: http://www.cbo.gov/ftpdocs/122xx/doc12212/06-21-Long-Term_Budget_Outlook.pdf

Council of Economic Advisors (2011a). *Economic report of the President: Main page*. Retrieved on August 13, 2011, from: http://www.gpoaccess.gov/eop/

Council of Economic Advisors (2011b). *Economic indicators: Main page*. Retrieved August 13, 2011, from: http://www.gpoaccess.gov/indicators/index.html

Energy Information Administration (2011a). *Petroleum & other liquids data*. Retrieved August 11, 2011, from: http://www.eia.gov/petroleum/data.cfm#prices

Energy Information Administration (2011b). *Weekly petroleum status report*. Retrieved August 12, 2011, from: http://www.eia.gov/oil_gas/petroleum/data_publications/weekly_petroleum_status_report/wpsr.html

Energy Information Administration (2011c). *Weekly natural gas storage report*. Retrieved August 12, 2011, from: http://ir.eia.gov/ngs/ngs.html

Federal Home Loan Bank of San Francisco (2011). *11th district cost of funds indices.* Retrieved August 11, 2011, from: http://www.fhlbsf.com/cofi/default.asp

Federal Reserve Bank of Philadelphia (2011). *Business outlook survey.* Retrieved August 10, 2011, from: http://www.philadelphiafed.org/research-and-data/regional-economy/business-outlook-survey/

Federal Reserve Bank of St. Louis (2011). *Federal reserve economic data—FRED.* Retrieved August 13, 2011, from: http://research.stlouisfed.org/fred2/

Financial Management Service (2011). *Current issue: Monthly treasury statement.* Retrieved August 13, 2011, from: http://www.fms.treas.gov/mts/index.html

Friedman, M. & Schwartz, A. (1963). *A monetary history of the United States, 1867–1960.* Princeton: Princeton University Press.

Goodhart, C (1975). Monetary relationships: The view from Threadneedle Street. In *Papers in monetary economics* (vol. i). Sydney: Reserve Bank of Australia.

Institute for Supply Management (2011). *ISM—ISM reports on business.* Retrieved August 10, 2011, from: http://www.ism.ws/ismreport/

Inter-Agency Group on Economic & Financial Statistics (2011). *Principal global indicators.* Retrieved August 13, 2011, from: http://www.principalglobalindicators.org/default.aspx

International Monetary Fund (2011). *IMF data and statistics.* Retrieved August 13, 2011, from: http://www.imf.org/external/data.htm

Investopedia (2011). *What is the quantity theory of money?.* Retrieved August 13, 2011, from: http://www.investopedia.com/articles/05/010705.asp#axzz1Uwb9GNoT

Keynes, J. M. (1936). *The general theory of employment, interest, and money.* Basingstoke, UK: Palgrave Macmillan.

Lucas, R. (1976). Economic policy evaluation: A critique. In K. Brunner & A. Meltzer (Eds.), *The Phillips curve and labor markets* (pp. 19–46, Carnegie-Rochester Conference Series on Public Policy, 1). New York: American Elsevier.

Microsoft (2011). *Economic data calendar: investing—MSN money.* Retrieved August 13, 2011, from: http://moneycentral.msn.com/investor/calendar/econ/current.asp

Monster Worldwide (2011). *Monster employment index.* Retrieved August 12, 2011, from: http://about-monster.com/employment-index

National Agriculture Statistics Service (2011). *Agricultural prices.* Retrieved August 11, 2011, from: http://usda.mannlib.cornell.edu/MannUsda/viewDocumentInfo.do?documentID=1002

National Association of Realtors (2011). *The NBER's business cycle dating procedure: Frequently asked questions.* Retrieved August 9, 2011, from: http://www.nber.org/cycles/recessions_faq.html

National Bureau of Economic Research (2011). *Real estate sales statistics.* Retrieved August 11, 2011, from: http://www.realtor.org/research/research/ehspage

Standard & Poors (2011). *S&P/Case—Shiller home price indices*. Retrieved August 11, 2011, from: http://www.standardandpoors.com/indices/sp-case-shiller-home-price-indices/en/us/?indexId=spusa-cashpidff--p-us----

Stengel, D. & Chaffe-Stengel, P. (forthcoming). *Working with time series data: Analysis and forecasting*. New York, NY: Business Expert Press.

Surowiecki, J. (2005). *The wisdom of crowds*. New York, NY: Anchor Books.

Thomson Reuters (2011). *Reuters/University of Michigan surveys of consumers*. Retrieved August 10, 2011, from: http://thomsonreuters.com/products_services/financial/financial_products/a-z/umichigan_surveys_of_consumers/#tab1

TreasuryDirect (2011a). *Institutional—How treasury auctions work*. Retrieved August 11, 2011, from: http://www.treasurydirect.gov/instit/auctfund/work/work.htm

TreasuryDirect (2011b). *Debt to the penny*. Retrieved August 13, 2011, from: http://www.treasurydirect.gov/NP/BPDLogin?application=np

U.S. Census Bureau (2011a). *Monthly & annual retail trade*. Retrieved August 9, 2011, from: http://www.census.gov/retail

U.S. Census Bureau (2011b). *Monthly & annual retail trade—Definitions*. Retrieved August 9, 2011, from: http://www.census.gov/retail/definitions.html

U.S. Census Bureau (2011c). *Quarterly retail e-commerce sales*. Retrieved August 9, 2011, from: http://www.census.gov/retail/mrts/www/data/pdf/ec_current.pdf

U.S. Census Bureau (2011d). *U.S. Census Bureau manufacturers' shipments, inventories, and orders*. Retrieved August 10, 2011, from: http://www.census.gov/manufacturing/m3/

U.S. Census Bureau (2011e). *New residential construction index*. Retrieved August 10, 2011, from: http://www.census.gov/const/www/newresconstindex.html

U.S. Census Bureau (2011f). *Construction spending*. Retrieved August 10, 2011, from: http://www.census.gov/const/www/c30index.html

U.S. Census Bureau (2011g). *Poverty*. Retrieved August 10, 2011, from: http://www.census.gov/newsroom/releases/archives/poverty/

U.S. Census Bureau (2011h). *New residential sales index*. Retrieved August 11, 2011, from: http://www.census.gov/const/www/newressalesindex.html

U.S. Census Bureau (2011i). *Manufacturing and trade inventories and sales*. Retrieved August 12, 2011, from: http://www.census.gov/mtis/

U.S. Department of Labor (2011). *ETA press release: Unemployment insurance weekly claims report*. Retrieved August 12, 2011, from: http://www.dol.gov/opa/media/press/eta/ui/current.htm

U.S. Department of the Treasury (2011a). *Treasury international capital system (TIC)—Home page*. Retrieved August 12, 2011, from: http://www.treasury.gov/resource-center/data-chart-center/tic/Pages/index.aspx

U.S. Department of the Treasury (2011b). *Current issue: Treasury bulletin.* Retrieved August 13, 2011, from: http://www.fms.treas.gov/bulletin/index. html

The Wall Street Journal (2011a). *Economic calendar—Market data center.* Retrieved August 13, 2011, from: http://online.wsj.com/mdc/public/ page/2_3063-economicCalendar.html?mod=mdc_h_cmgrel

The Wall Street Journal (2011b). *Economic indicators archive—Market data center.* Retrieved August 13, 2011, from: http://online.wsj.com/mdc/public/ page/2_3024-indicate.html?mod=topnav_2_3063

The World Bank (2011a). *Poverty analysis—Measuring inequality.* Retrieved August 10, 2011, from: http://web.worldbank.org/WBSITE/EXTERNAL/ TOPICS/EXTPOVERTY/EXTPA/0,,contentMDK:20238991~menuPK:4 92138~pagePK:148956~piPK:216618~theSitePK:430367,00.html

The World Bank (2011b). *Data|The world bank.* Retrieved August 13, 2011, from: http://data.worldbank.org/

Yahoo! (2011). *Economic calendar.* Retrieved August 13, 2011, from: http://biz. yahoo.com/c/e.html

Index

Announcing the Business Expert Press Digital Library

Concise E-books Business Students Need for Classroom and Research

This book can also be purchased in an e-book collection by your library as

- a one-time purchase,
- that is owned forever,
- allows for simultaneous readers,
- has no restrictions on printing, and
- can be downloaded as PDFs from within the library community.

Our digital library collections are a great solution to beat the rising cost of textbooks. E-books can be loaded into their course management systems or onto student's e-book readers.

The **Business Expert Press** digital libraries are very affordable, with no obligation to buy in future years.

For more information, please visit **www.businessexpertpress.com/librarians**. To set up a trial in the United States, please contact **Sheri Dean** at *sheri.dean@globalpress.com*; for all other regions, contact **Nicole Lee** at *nicole.lee@igroupnet.com*.

OTHER TITLES IN OUR ECONOMICS AND FINANCE COLLECTION
Collection Editor: **Philip J. Romero and Jeffrey A. Edwards**

Managerial Economics: Concepts and Principles by Donald N. Stengel

Your Macroeconomic Edge: Investing Strategies for the Post-Recession World by Philip J. Romero

CPSIA information can be obtained at www.ICGtesting.com
Printed in the USA
BVOW020620120912

300038BV00006B/1/P

9 781606 492826